HERE'S WHAT READERS HAVE SAID ABOUT

THE HURTING PARENT

T0048896

"I can't tell you how I've searched for such a book—a comforting, encouraging, inspiring word to Christian parents whose children have rebelled. How I wish I could have had the help from your book when I was waiting on those long, endless nights. But I'm thankful I have it now, for my daughter isn't yet in the fold and there are still some anxious moments."

"Reading *The Hurting Parent* was a real ministry to my wife and me in our time of family trauma."

"I read *The Hurting Parent* and immediately ordered five copies for relatives who hurt. My husband, who is a college sociology professor, is going to recommend it for reading in his Marriage and Family class."

"I wish I could have had access to such a book years ago. It would have been helpful in dealing with so many families in my parishes through the years."

"We will always cherish this book and read it again and again on days we feel discouraged."

"My wife and I have been going through a particularly difficult period the last few years because of anorexia, an eating disorder that has gripped two of our children. Our daughter attempted suicide twice. Our son has been close several times. Your book has provided both comfort and guidance."

"Thank you for writing *The Hurting Parent*. I use it as a helpful tool in my work for a mental health agency where I counsel many hurting parents."

"Recently I've been on the brink of complete despair. This book has given me new hope as it will many others."

"Our thirteen-year-old daughter has worried us to death. She read my copy of *The Hurting Parent* and with tears in her eyes told me, 'I'll never run away again.'"

"I've appreciated the book even though I'm not a hurting parent. I can relate as a child and appreciate my parents even more."

"Your subject matter in *The Hurting Parent* could not be more pertinent. My days and nights, as a pastor, are filled with the needs of hurting, brokenhearted parents."

"I found it to be an emotional book that made me feel I belonged to a great company of hurting people for whom you were offering comfort, guidance, encouragement, and hope."

"I have read many Christian books and have yet to find one with such honest insight and encouragement for suffering parents. (And there are many of us.) I've already recommended the book to three pastors and two youth leaders, and have personally given away four copies to hurting parents and a counselor with the juvenile court."

"I read the book recently and want to thank you. It came to us in the final stage of our crisis. Our unmarried daughter had her baby two days ago."

"I have just finished reading *The Hurting Parent* cover to cover for the second time. The first time I read it I went back to the bookstore and bought four more copies to give away. We have twelve children and have been through 90 percent of the situations covered in your book. It has given me much encouragement and support."

"At a flea market, I happened across a table of used paperbacks with your book on it. I was so desperate for some kind of answer to the painful relationship I have with my son that I bought it and started reading right there. That book was like a gift from God himself. It was as if he planted it there for me to find in my time of need. It truly was a miracle for me. I have read it twice and loaned it to a friend. When it wasn't returned to me after nine months, I bought another copy to read for the third time. But I couldn't start it again without dropping you a line to thank you for this wonderful gift. My problems are far from over. But at least now I know I'm not going crazy. And I'm not alone."

THE
HURTING
PARENT

THE
HURTING
PARENT

UPDATED AND EXPANDED

HELP AND HOPE
FOR PARENTS OF PRODIGALS

MARGIE M. LEWIS
WITH
GREGG LEWIS

ZONDERVAN.com/
AUTHORTRACKER
follow your favorite authors

ZONDERVAN

The Hurting Parent
Copyright © 1980, 1988 by Margie M. Lewis and Gregg Lewis
Copyright © 2009 by Gregg Lewis and Mark E. Lewis

Requests for information should be addressed to:

Zondervan, *Grand Rapids, Michigan* 49530

Library of Congress Cataloging-in-Publication Data

Lewis, Margie M., 1923–
　　The hurting parent : help and hope for parents of prodigals / Margie M. Lewis with
　Gregg Lewis. – [Updated and expanded ed.].
　　　　p.　cm.
　　Includes bibliographical references.
　　ISBN 978-0-310-28661-5 (softcover : alk. paper)
　　1. Families – Religious life. 2. Parent and child – Religious aspects – Christianity.
　3. Problem children. I. Lewis, Gregg, 1951– II. Title.
　BV4529.L48　2010
　248.8'45 – dc22　　　　　　　　　　　　　　　　　　　　　　2009040182

Cover design: Jeff Gifford
Interior design: Michelle Espinoza

Printed in the United States of America

10 11 12 13 14 15 • 25 24 23 22 21 20 19 18 17 16 15 14 13 12 11 10 9 8 7 6 5 4 3 2 1

To my loving sons and daughters-in-law—
Mack, Mark and Angela, Gregg and Deborah
—and my ten grandchildren.

And to Ralph,
my dear husband of fifty-three years,
who lived long enough to see and rejoice with me
over the beginning of "the rest of the story."

CONTENTS

PREFACE

In Love's service only the wounded soldiers can serve.
— Thornton Wilder

UPDATED AND EXPANDED EDITION

Time and its passage always seem to surprise us — no matter how much of it we have experienced. Indeed, much has changed since I helped my mother write the original edition of this book three decades ago.

The seed idea for the book was planted when Mom sent me a letter asking me to pray with her for a friend of hers whose son was a drug addict. The letter prompted me not only to pray for this mother and son, but to think about a number of Christian parents I knew who anguished over their sons and daughters.

As editor of *Campus Life* magazine at that time, I was unaware of anything written on the subject. But since I wasn't yet a parent myself at that point, I didn't feel I had either the right or the wisdom to write on the subject. Yet I had witnessed my parents' hurt when my brother Mark distanced himself from our family and faith; I had seen them work at rebuilding a relationship with Mark; and I knew my parents' experience had sensitized them to the feelings of other parents who felt hurt for their children. So I wrote to my mother to suggest we work together on this book.

Convinced from the start that *The Hurting Parent* could meet a crying need and provide a valuable ministry, we wrote what I considered at the time to be a modest little book. But we've been amazed at the magnitude of the response. Although *The Hurting Parent* remains one of the simplest, shortest books I've ever written, I daresay none of the fifty-some books I've authored or coauthored since have had as broad, as personally rewarding, or (certainly) as long a ministry as has this. The Lord has chosen to use it in some remarkable and very unexpected ways.

I never would have imagined an updated and expanded edition of this book thirty years after its beginning. Yet the title has not only stayed in print all this time, but has kept right on selling (with more than 250,000 copies in print) and ministering to a steady stream of readers who have continued to share their own stories and heartaches with us over the years. From the time it first rolled off the press right up until recent weeks, the ongoing responses this book has elicited from famous Christian leaders and ordinary Christians alike has heartened and humbled us. Only a month or so ago I corresponded on another subject with the longtime publisher at a different Christian publishing house who requested of me, "If you think of it when you [next] talk with your mother, please give her my greetings. I still think her work on *The Hurting Parent* was among the most courageous I've seen in my years of publishing. It was not usual in those times to talk about the struggles of one's family, and certainly not in conservative Christian circles, and even less among Christian leaders. It was a pioneering work, and I believe God honored her courage and faithfulness by bringing Mark to himself."

Yes, much has changed in the time that has passed since the previous editions of this book. My "prodigal" brother, who is now as old as my mother was when she and I first worked on *The Hurting Parent*, is in a far different (and we might add far nearer) place—both physically and spiritually—than he was thirty years ago. We'll share more about that in the pages that follow.

Time has changed things for Mom as well. Her advancing age, along with physical limitations and the death of her husband (after more than fifty years of marriage) has long since brought an end to her public ministry of speaking and leading seminars on this subject around the country. Yet she still regularly corresponds or talks by phone with a number of hurting parents—some of whom she has been counseling and whose children she has cared and prayed for since this book was first published.

This is one of the reasons she has been excited about this updated and expanded edition and the opportunity to provide input.

What thirty years of passing time has not changed very much is the hurting parent experience, and my mom's compassion and concern for those with whom she has shared it. Just last month she and I received heart-wrenching news from a woman very dear to both of us. She reported that her daughter, whom we'd known and loved from birth, had recently walked away from her husband and her infant son to take up with another man. She is now filing for divorce. And her hurting parents are searching for any encouragement they can find.

Truth be told, I'm afraid more people today than ever before need the help and the hope *The Hurting Parent* has provided countless thousands of readers and their families for thirty years now. That is why this special edition contains everything that was in the previous versions — and more. We've even included my mother's original preface here, which I encourage you to read for a fuller understanding of our motives and goals for writing. You'll find scattered additions and updates throughout the original twelve chapters. And finally, in the new chapters closing out this edition, you can read an update on Mom's own hurting parent experience. We think you'll agree it's a rather remarkable "rest of the story" — a conclusion that would have been inconceivable thirty years ago.

As you begin to read, let us say once again that we thank God for the way the previous versions of this book have already been used. We hope this updated and expanded edition will broaden its impact as it ministers to the needs of even more hurting Christian parents. And we pray God may use what our family has experienced, learned, and written to speak to and sensitize all those who read what follows.

— Gregg Lewis, Summer 2009

FIRST EDITION

For a number of years I have been looking for a book that would speak to or about Christian parents who hurt for their non-Christian children. Perhaps the Christian community has been reluctant to admit Christian families also face struggles and heartache. Or maybe Christian publishers haven't realized how many thousands of us hurting Christian parents there are. Whatever the reasons, I have never found a book that captured the emotions and pain hurting parents feel.

I could walk into any Christian bookstore and buy half a truckload of books on the Christian family. I could find a wealth of very practical how-to books covering almost every subject imaginable — from discipline to devotions and from creative coloring to the covenantal family. It seems every Christian psychologist and half the ministers in North America have recorded their advice on how we can successfully raise our children in the nurture of the Lord and see them joyously line up behind us to march in the great army of Christ.

But what can we do if we didn't read these books until it was too late? What can we do if we followed all those principles and guidelines for Christian parenthood and they just didn't seem to work? What can we do if we made parenting mistakes that were too serious or too long ago to correct now? What can we do if we have no idea what (if anything) we did wrong? What do we do when our teenage or young adult children go AWOL from the ranks of believers and decide to march to the beat of the world and its forces?

I have yet to find a book that tackles these questions. So what follows is my attempt to fill a great gap on bookstore racks and on church library shelves. I'm writing to those who are more interested in the "what now?" questions than in how-to advice. And my primary goal is to encourage hurting parents by helping them understand their reactions and by providing them with survival strategies tested in the experiences of other parents who have known their pain.

Hurting parents, however, make up only one of the audiences I have had in mind as I have written this book. There are two more.

Hurting parents need the encouragement and support of others. Yet acquaintances, friends, and even relatives often have no understanding of what hurting parents are going through.

This problem hit me especially hard during an interview I had with a mother who told me about the anguish she feels for her alcoholic son. I remembered him years ago as a teenager, when I, like other Christian adults who watched him grow up, had been so judgmental, so lacking in sympathy. I had concentrated my condemning concern on his actions, giving little consideration to him as a person, and even less to his heart-broken parents. As I listened to this mother's voice break as she talked about the pain and the loneliness she felt during those years, I had to weep with remorse at my own past insensitivity. I couldn't help wondering what difference it would have made if I and a few others had reached out to that boy and his parents when they first began to hurt.

I went home from that interview praying that what I wrote could help prevent such tragedies. I would hope that after reading this book, anyone who is not a hurting parent could better empathize with, understand, and help those who are.

My third target audience is made up of Christian leaders—counselors, speakers, and especially pastors. The importance of this segment of readers was emphasized graphically by one hurting mother who read the first draft of this book. She said, "If Christian ministers are going to be good shepherds, they need to be on the lookout for hurting sheep. You can't expect an injured sheep to come running for help. A shepherd has to go to hurting sheep and understand the problem before he can begin to care for them."

So to pastors I hope this book bleats loudly enough to call attention to the plight of many hurting sheep who suffer silently and uncomforted. I hope the cry is clear enough to give understanding to shepherds so they can better care for the hurting parents in their flocks.

I realize my three-pronged audience is broad. And I know the goals I have stated here are big goals. But the need is great. I can only pray God will use what I have learned and written to speak to and sensitize all those who read what follows.

—Margie M. Lewis, Spring 1979

ACKNOWLEDGMENTS

First, I would like to express my deepest gratitude to all the hurting parents, the wounded soldiers, who bared their hearts and their hurts to me during the preparation of the original version of this book. They did so unselfishly in order that others may be helped. (Their names have been changed to protect their privacy and that of their families.)

I am humbled by, and indebted to, the countless readers who have responded to the earlier editions of *The Hurting Parent*. Their stories and the opportunity to interact with them over the last thirty years has strengthened me and improved the subsequent versions of this book.

Also deserving many thanks are those advisers and friends who have assisted and encouraged me by reading and discussing what is written here.

Of course, this book never would have been possible without the loving support of my husband, Ralph, and of my family during the long months of labor on the manuscript. Special thanks go to my son Mark for all I've learned through him and from him, for his permission to write about the experiences we have shared, and for relating the rest of the story in this latest edition.

A large measure of appreciation is also due my son Gregg, who first proposed we do this book together. He has taken my ideas, my experiences, and the materials I have gathered and helped mold them into a cohesive whole.

Finally, I want to thank my heavenly Father, the first hurting parent, whose all-powerful presence, understanding, grace, and love have been my strength for these past thirty years. And longer.

—Margie M. Lewis

CHAPTER 1

INITIATION

Happy families are all alike;
every unhappy family is unhappy in its own way.
—Tolstoy, *Anna Karenina*

I set the supper table for five, as usual. But Mark wasn't home, so we waited. A few minutes passed before I finally called my husband and my other two sons. As we prayed and began the meal without Mark, I felt the first tinge of apprehension.

His absence at lunch hadn't concerned me. A college sophomore's days are often busy and unpredictable. Besides, he had ridden his new motorcycle to campus that morning, and the sunny November election day warmed to a gorgeous afternoon for riding. But it was out of character for Mark to skip supper without leaving a word.

By the time we had finished the meal and I had cleared the table and stuck a plate of leftovers in the oven to stay warm, I couldn't help indulging in a little motherly worry. When I left a few minutes later for an evening sewing class I was thinking to myself, *I hope he hasn't gotten hurt on that motorcycle.*

I hurried home after class with an anxiety any mother of a teenage motorcyclist could appreciate. "Is he home yet?" I asked as my husband met me at the door. Ralph shook his head and led me to a seat on the couch.

"Mark won't be home tonight," Ralph said. "He left this morning for Florida." Ralph went on to explain that he had talked to a friend who had learned Mark's plans that morning, just before Mark left town on his heavily loaded Honda. I couldn't believe what I was hearing.

He's gone. My mind churned over the implications of that thought. *Florida? Why? Why didn't he tell us? He has probably turned around by now and is heading home. He could be back anytime now. Of course it's going to be all right—isn't it?*

Hours later we went to bed. And there, between my husband's racking sobs and my own prayers for Mark's safety and return, I listened to the stillness of the night. Finally, I heard it. The sound of that approaching motorcycle was joyous music to my ears. Closer. Closer. Then … no. Just the roar of another biker passing.

I dozed fitfully through the long darkness, waking often to the sound of continued silence. When the morning sunlight finally broke through the bedroom windows, we rose and went through the motions of a day.

Night fell again. We placed a call to one of Mark's old friends at Georgia Tech. Yes, the friend told us, Mark was there. He had stopped on his way south.

What a relief it was to hear Mark's voice. He wouldn't say much. We were glad to know he wasn't depressed. But we were distressed to learn he was going on with his trip.

When we hung up, the questions again filled my mind. *Why wouldn't he explain? What had we done? What had we said? Oh God, why?*

We checked his desk and looked under pillows. We sorted through wastebaskets. But we found no note, no answers. Of course, I knew thousands of teenagers leave home unannounced every year. But why an independent nineteen-year-old like Mark? We called the bank; he had withdrawn only a small sum from his savings account. Why did he leave in the middle of a college term? Did he have grade problems? Was he in trouble on campus? Dozens of questions had answers of no. But most of our questions had no answers at all.

Time passed. Each new day brought renewed hope and added disappointment. Every morning I waited anxiously for the postman then flipped quickly through the mail, searching for a card, a word. Days soon added up to weeks. Still nothing. Thanksgiving Day came and went.

One mid-December morning I rifled fruitlessly through the mail. Then, as I opened a credit card statement, I saw where Mark had bought two dollars worth of gas. Three and a half weeks before, he had been alive in Florida.

When Ralph came home for lunch, we pulled out a map and pinpointed the spot. A credit card charge wasn't much, but it was something. And it bolstered our spirits.

Hope soared again a few days later with an early morning phone call. An old family friend reported that his daughter had seen our son near West Palm Beach. Mark had told her he was working in a motel there and asked her not to contact us. But when she had told her father, he had insisted on telling us.

A motel. Near West Palm Beach. Again the news wasn't much. But it was enough. Someone had seen him and actually talked to him. He was okay.

Months before, our family had planned a holiday vacation at my parents' home in Florida. And in questioning Mark's friends, we learned he had said something to one of them about taking a bike trip to Florida and meeting his family for Christmas. So we continued with our plans.

I carefully wrapped our presents with more than the usual holiday anticipation. This year Christmas would hold extra meaning for our family; we would all be together again.

Every mile down the interstate brought us closer to that reunion. The why of his leaving didn't seem to matter much anymore. *His return would be enough*, I told myself. If he could only know that. But we had nowhere to send the message. *Oh God, make him realize how much we love him.*

If Mark was indeed working at a motel during this peak tourist season, we probably couldn't expect him at his grandparents' until

Christmas Day. But once we were in Florida, we were content to wait a few more days.

When Christmas finally dawned into a beautiful Florida winter day, the family agreed to delay the gift-giving and the turkey meal until late afternoon. We wanted Mark to have plenty of time to cover the two hundred miles that still separated us.

Again we listened for the sound of the bike. We heard nothing, however, but passing cars and the laughter of young children playing in the sun with their brand-new toys.

Inside it was quiet. Midafternoon we reluctantly agreed to open our presents. And later, after a tearful Christmas prayer, I tried to force myself to eat a tasteless turkey dinner. When the long, draining day came to an end, a half dozen packages remained unopened beneath the tree.

Three days of heartsick waiting followed. It was time to head for home. But we determined not to leave Florida without one last desperate try at contact. So instead of starting north, we journeyed south and east across the state toward West Palm Beach.

But one stop at a roadside telephone booth dashed most of our hope. West Palm Beach was surrounded with yellow page after yellow page of motels. We didn't even know where to begin.

Dozens of fruitless calls later we resorted to driving up and down the palm-lined streets, stopping at motel after motel. The scenes in the motel offices soon became an anguished routine. A finger pointed to the middle of a family portrait. "Have you seen this boy? He's my son. He's working somewhere around here in a motel." Time after time the answer was no or a sad shake of the head.

Exposing such personal hurt to strangers was torture. But almost always there was an encouraging response: "If I see him, I'll tell him you were here," or "I'll have him contact you if he shows up here." Strangers were moved by a family picture and a parent's love.

As the day wore on, we went back to the phones. Calling was much faster, even if it was not more productive.

Late in the afternoon our continuing prayers met with an air of peace. All four of us in the car felt it. We were ready to surrender the day and start home. It was time to go. But first, one last street — a concession to undying hope.

I don't remember who saw it first. "Over there! Stop! There's a motorcycle at that motel! It's his license!"

My heart raced with the excitement of eight long weeks of pent-up hope and worry. At long last we had found our son. We had no plans to snatch him or force him to come home. We just wanted to see him and let him know how much we still loved him. And this was the chance we had longed for.

Ralph got out and knocked at the office door. The manager pointed him toward the rear of the premises. The rest of us waited in the car. Ralph disappeared through a workshop door. Minutes passed before he emerged again. And there was Mark, a tall, tanned figure in the doorway. They were talking.

As more minutes passed, I watched every movement, waiting for my cue to leave the car and greet my son. But the cue never came. Mark stepped back out of view, and Ralph turned and walked slowly, head down, back to the car.

What was wrong?

Mark hadn't wanted to be found. Ralph had shared our love. But Mark wanted us to leave.

Beneath the tears I had the thought, *Maybe our love is too much for him right now. God knows my love is more than I can handle.*

We respected Mark's wishes and his personhood. And we drove away, onto the northbound interstate, headed for home. Outside I cried. Inside I hurt as I had never hurt before.

I begin this book with these personal experiences because they served as my initiation rites into a fraternity of people I have termed "hurting parents." These incidents marked the start of what became a painful, years-long process of struggle, growth, and reconciliation that has affected every area of my life and the life of my family.

Pain seems to be part of the job requirement for parents. Parenthood begins with the gripping pain of labor and delivery. Then, as their little ones develop, caring mothers and fathers vicariously experience every pain and hurt their children face — from scraped knees and bloodied noses to disease and sometimes even death. As their offspring grow, parents suffer the agony of watching and letting them blunder through the initial stages of independence. And those parents who survive the physical and emotional cuts and bruises of childhood and adolescence feel another kind of pain when they finally cut the umbilical cord of adulthood and see their grown-up child step out on his or her own. All these pains are normal; they come with the territory of parenthood.

But the parents this book is for and about know a different, deeper kind of hurt. In short, hurting parents are those who feel they have failed at their divinely appointed task of Christian parenthood. They have attempted to fulfill their biblical injunction to "train up a child in the way he should go." They have worked to build family unity on a firm foundation of Christian faith and to teach their families love and obedience toward God.

These parents are crushed when one of their children casts off those family ties. They are heartbroken when a son rejects some or all of the Christian values or standards of living they labored so hard to instill. Or they are devastated when a daughter abandons the Christian faith they always tried to teach and live.

The hurt may set in when a son runs away from home without leaving any word of explanation or when a sobbing fifteen-year-old daughter admits her pregnancy. The pain may begin with a child's involvement in a non-Christian lifestyle — drugs, a strange religious cult, living with a boyfriend or girlfriend before marriage. A high schooler may resist going to church with claims of boredom or lack of relevance. An undergrad exposed to the new intellectual atmosphere of college may question or even feel he has outgrown his parents' beliefs. The hurt could be prompted by something as shocking as an announcement of homosexuality or as gradual and common as a case of a growing adolescent's rebellion.

The crisis point varies from family to family. But the results are always the same—parents hurt with the frustration of what they see as their own failure. And they judge themselves guilty with the constant question: What did I do wrong?

They start to take unusual notice of the seemingly ideal families that surround them in their church or community—the Smiths, whose son is a university honor student with plans to become a medical missionary to Africa, or the Joneses' eighteen-year-old twin daughters who sang a duet in church Sunday right after they shared how much they appreciated family devotions in their home. When hurting parents compare their own problems with those of families like the Smiths and the Joneses, they can't help wondering, *What's wrong with our family? Why does this have to happen to us, to our family?*

There is an embarrassing feeling of unique aloneness that Tolstoy summed up perfectly in the first sentence of Anna Karenina. "Happy families are all alike; every unhappy family is unhappy in its own way." Every hurting parent does face a personal crisis as different as the personalities involved; so there may be some justification for those feelings of differentness. But any parent who thinks his or her anguish is unique, that he holds the monopoly on parental pain or that no one else could possibly understand the heartbreak she is going through, is absolutely mistaken.

I have to confess I felt some of that same sense of aloneness in those months after Mark left home. And even after I had known and shared with a number of hurting parents and had begun to think about this book, I wondered if there were really enough hurting Christian parents out there to warrant the effort. But it seemed everyone I approached about the possibility of a book like this was a hurting parent, or knew two or three they felt I should interview.

After scores of those interviews with parents from all parts of the country, after numerous discussions with pastors, counselors, and Christian psychologists, and now after all the feedback I have received from the earlier editions of *The Hurting Parent*, I'm convinced beyond the shadow of any doubt that the hurting-parent problem is common to every church and community. It began with Adam and Eve when Cain killed Abel. And there seems to be no lessening of the problem here in the twenty-first century.

I have found young hurting parents whose junior highers were just beginning to rebel against parental authority. And I discovered hurting senior citizen parents whose non-Christian middle-aged children still give them cause for sadness and concern. The family circumstances and the causes vary greatly. But the parental self-doubt and hurt are always there.

One day not long ago an old friend, a pastor's wife visiting in our town, stopped to see me. We talked for a while about people we knew. She asked about my family, and then I asked about hers. "I'm about to become a grandmother for the first time," she said.

Normally, my automatic and happy response would be a hearty "Congratulations!" I didn't say anything, however, as she went on with pain in her voice to add, "But I don't want to be a grandmother. Not like this." And she went on to tell me that her teenage son and his girlfriend (whose family were members of her husband's parish) had to get married. The baby was due before long, and she said, "I don't know how I can go on."

A high school teacher, a respected member of his local church, told me about the night he and his wife got a phone call from a policeman in another state. "He couldn't have hit us with his billy club any harder than he did with those words: 'We've got your son here in our jail. He's charged as a juvenile for carrying a concealed weapon.'"

"We felt as if the bottoms of our hearts dropped out and all the feelings fell through," the father said. "We couldn't even cry."

A few years ago I received a letter from a new Christian, a woman who had been, in her own words, "the most hated, most wanted person in my town." She had peddled pot to the local teenagers. She was known to everyone for miles around as a boozer and could have handily won a countywide election for "worst mother of the year." But after this newly converted mother's teenage son ended up in jail one night for a drunken rampage, she wrote me about her anguish. "I felt as if everything in me died," she said. "I hated him for what he'd done and loved him at the same time. And I cried for days."

The pain is the same—for despised and respected families alike.

In fact, whether they deserve it or not, ministers' families are notorious for problem children. Maybe the reason is that preachers' kids are always held up as examples—good and bad. Whatever the explanation, most of us know of ministers whose offspring don't practice what the parents preach. Consider a moment the frustration and the pain of pastors and pastors' spouses who see their children ignore, reject, and sometimes even trample on the standards and the beliefs to which they as parents have dedicated their lives. In their hurt, they more than anyone must wonder why.

Yet it is not the purpose of this book to try to answer the "What did I do wrong?" or the "Why did this happen to us?" questions. Hurting parents don't need to dwell on mistakes they may have made in the past or on steps they might have taken. They already hurt. They need to know: "Where do I go from here? What can be done now to redeem the situation? How can I win my son or my daughter back to our family and to God?"

Those are the answers we will be looking for in the disguised but true stories of the hurting parents who share their experiences, their feelings, and their advice in the following chapters. I hope that by reading what these people have learned about themselves, about their children, and about God, you, too, will discover what God has to say to and through hurting Christian parents.

SOMETHING TO THINK ABOUT

At the end of each chapter in the second edition of this book we added a few questions designed for use by hurting-parent support groups or by classes using this book. The questions are intended merely as starting points for further thinking and discussion of the hurting-parent experience. Chapters could be read and discussed one at a time. Or since the chapters alternately deal with negative and positive reactions, there could be some advantage in reading and discussing some of the chapters in pairs—chapters 2 and 3, 4 and 5, 6 and 7, 8 and 9, and 10 and 11.

1. What are some of the "normal" pains of parenthood you have experienced or witnessed?

2. What emotions do you think the various hurting Christian parents in this chapter feel? What other emotions might hurting parents feel?

3. What biblical hurting parents can you think of? Make a list.

4. Try to imagine the feelings of a hurting parent you know. Pray silently and specifically for that hurting parent and his or her child.

CHAPTER 2

ISOLATION

Bitter shame hath spoiled the sweet world's taste,
that it yields nought but shame and bitterness.
—*Shakespeare*, King John

Marcie Klein's mind wandered far from her regular housework. *Oh God, you must know where my son is today*, she thought as she lifted a lamp and swished her dust cloth over the end table. *He's probably so strung out on dope that even he doesn't know where he is. Please, Lord, help him.*

The desperate words of prayer turned to bitterness as Marcie's thoughts shifted to her daughter. *Maybe it's easier to know nothing. Knowing where my daughter is certainly doesn't make things any better … living with no-good trash in that dump of a building. Why, God? Why does—*

The welcome ringing of the phone broke through Marcie's clouded thoughts. She was glad for anything to occupy her mind a few minutes—any temporary diversion from the constant worry that plagued her days.

The caller was Carol Phillips, an old friend, who wanted to know if Marcie and her husband, Jim, could come for dinner the following week. Marcie agreed.

But as the time approached, Marcie began to dread the evening. The Phillipses' two sons gave their folks nothing but pride; one taught in a local high school and the other planned to enter the ministry when he graduated from seminary at the end of the year. Marcie felt like a failure in comparison. The last thing on earth she wanted to do was to go to dinner at the Phillipses' and have to talk about families.

Yet we do have a lot of other things in common, Marcie told herself. *And it would be good to get out and forget my own problems.*

By the time Marcie and Jim rang the Phillipses' doorbell, she had talked herself out of most of her apprehension. Tom Phillips opened the door and ushered them into the living room. There on the couch were two other dinner guests, Alan and Doris Nicholson, longtime mutual friends of the Kleins and the Phillipses. The Nicholsons' presence pleased Marcie—it would mean even more to talk about at dinner.

Everything started smoothly. The three couples reminisced about old times and acquaintances. The company of friends seemed the perfect therapy for Marcie. Tom Phillips told a couple of funny stories, and Marcie laughed for the first time in days.

It wasn't until halfway through the main course that Alan Nicholson asked Tom and Carol about their seminarian son. Tom briefly relayed the news from his son's most recent letter, but Alan kept the discussion alive.

"You must be proud of him," he said. "You ought to be proud of both your sons. I don't know what you did to raise two such outstanding Christian boys, but you must have done something right!"

As her friend continued his eloquent discourse on the merits of the Phillips boys, Marcie felt like shriveling into her seat. "Emotions of envy and humiliation almost overwhelmed me," she admitted. "It was all I could do to choke down my food and swallow my backed-up tears.

"I spent the next two hours fighting my feelings of shame and waiting impatiently for the first gracious opportunity to excuse myself and leave. After what seemed like an eternal evening, I finally walked out that door feeling like a pardoned prisoner.

"No sooner had I climbed in and shut my car door than I burst into tears. 'Why did we have to come?'

"Jim put a comforting arm around me and answered sadly, 'I don't know.' A few minutes later he started the car. All the way home we talked about how awkward and out of place we'd felt the entire night."

Many hurting parents have talked to me about the isolation of shame. Their reasons have varied from adult children whose drug dealing made statewide headlines to a high school freshman's conspicuous absence from his parents' pew on Sunday morning because he was bored with church. Yet no matter the cause, shamed parents use similar words and expressions to describe the feeling: embarrassment, humiliation, inferiority, incompetence, disgrace, loss of face. Often they express fear of rejection, disrespect, disapproval, contempt, and even pity from the people around them who witness their struggles.

I remember sitting in church one time after my son left home and thinking, *How is this going to look? Here my husband and I are our church's family-life coordinators and this happens in our home.*

Most of us who have children are victims of parental egos. Our children make up such an important part of our lives that we begin to draw much of our own identities from their lives and behavior. And we face a parental peer pressure, to be viewed as good parents, that is as strong or stronger than that adolescent peer pressure we experienced as youth. But this new peer pressure is complicated by the fact that our present status isn't just determined by our own reactions; it is also affected by our children. Their successes and accomplishments become feathers in our parental caps. Their mistakes, failures, and troubles become reason for our own very personal shame. And that shame is a common, understandable, yet troublesome trap into which many hurting parents fall.

Occasionally others' cruel attitudes prompt a parent's feeling of shame over a child. One such case was shared by a father I talked to. He and his wife had been struggling with their rebellious nineteen-year-old daughter for a couple of years. She had long since quit going to church with them. And her social life was far from what they could have approved of or wanted for her. But these parents were striving hard to maintain a loving relationship with their daughter.

"My wife and I went with our daughter to a large family reunion," the man said. "We all enjoyed the big meal and the chance to talk with relatives we hadn't seen since the reunion the year before.

"But as the long afternoon dragged on, my daughter's interest waned. She began to put pressure on us to head for home. The third time I put her off, she angrily blurted out a threat to take off with the car and leave us to find our own way home.

"One of my cousins who overheard this exchange ripped off his belt and handed it to me. He didn't say a word, but his meaning was as clear as the snide smile on his face: 'If you knew how to manage your daughter, you wouldn't be having all this trouble with her.'

"I knew the belt wasn't the answer, but I was so humiliated by my cousin's contempt that we escaped to our car within minutes and drove home."

Fortunately, such callousness is the exception, not the rule. More often a hurting parent's shame will be triggered by another's unthinking insensitivity, which is magnified by his or her own supersensitivity about a son or daughter. That is what happened to Marcie Klein in the dinner incident at the beginning of this chapter.

Another example occurred in my own Sunday school class some years ago. The week after our annual evangelistic campaign, one of the class members stood up to express his appreciation for the ministry of the evangelist. He commented on the preacher's fine messages and went on to laud the man's personal spiritual character. "But perhaps the greatest indication of our evangelist's Christian commitment and witness is his family," he continued. "His children are fine Christian young people; in fact, all three of them are engaged in some form of Christian service."

I winced at those words. Glancing around the room, I counted nearly a dozen dedicated Christian parents who besieged heaven daily with prayers of loving concern for the welfare and the souls of their non-Christian children.

No doubt our fellow class member had only meant to commend the evangelist. But not one of us hurting parents in the room could have missed the unspoken implication that a person's children are the most accurate measure of that parent's own spiritual character and condition.

I must confess there was a time in my life when I might have agreed with that. It is pretty easy to embark on a spiritual ego trip when all your children are in Sunday school, morning worship services, youth fellowship, and all the other right places we might want our sons and daughters to be. It is easy to sit in a church pew with your family, padding your own judgment seat with your "success" as a Christian parent and think, *It's too bad about some of these parents in our church who've missed the boat with their children. I wonder what turned their kids off. How can these people give such glowing testimonies?*

But I can't do that any longer, because I have sat in that other pew and because too many hurting Christian parents have won a place on my saint's list with their inspiring examples of Christlike love and patience. If that seems incongruous, think about God, the father model for all parents. Then look at his chosen children of Israel. God has watched his children wander and rebel since the beginning of time. Knowing that God understands comforts me.

It also convinces me that if a perfect heavenly Father can be a hurting parent, we ought to think twice before we judge the spirituality of ourselves or other human parents by the behavior or the faith of a son or daughter. Yet too many people still do it.

And the judgmental attitudes of meddling family members, insensitive friends, and perhaps even unthinking church members who feel they have exemplary Christian children can shame a hurting parent who is already experiencing the haunting fear of inadequacy as a mother or a father. Though the emotion of shame, however, is a reaction to such other people and their opinions, the feeling itself is a self-directed and often self-inflicted pain.

A longtime acquaintance surprised me recently when he told me about the shame he had felt when his son got into some trouble a few years ago. "I had to force myself to go to church," he said. "I desperately wanted to stay home and hide. At the amen of the benediction, I would slip out of my end spot on one of the back pews and make a beeline for the door. I'd look neither right nor left, hoping to seem so intent on some urgent deed that no one would dare intercept me before I reached the refuge of my car."

When I expressed my surprise and admitted my ignorance about the incident my friend had been so ashamed about, he couldn't believe it.

"I thought everyone in town knew about it," he said. The truth was, very few people knew the details. This father had just been so wrapped up in his own hurt he imagined everyone was scrutinizing him and his family. As a result, he suffered unnecessary self-imposed shame.

The feeling of being on exhibit, this idea that everyone in town or in church knows the particulars of your family problems and thinks you have failed as a parent is a self-defeating, often self-manufactured lie. But then, shame itself is a very self-centered emotion. I would even go so far as to say it closely borders on pride. Perhaps we are slow to recognize or admit the negative roots of shame because we so often confuse the feeling of humiliation with the admirable quality of humility.

Outwardly, shame and humility may result in similar characteristics. For example, both a humble person and a humiliated person will try to avoid the limelight of attention.

But the bases of humility and shame are very different, if not opposites. Humility grows from an outward concern, an attitude of putting others first. Shame, on the other hand, results directly from a concern for self and what others think of that self; it is pride pointed inward.

A hurting parent who is suffering shame certainly wouldn't feel proud; the usual characteristics we associate with pride (smugness, self-satisfaction, arrogance) are too easily broken, battered, and torn away like the branches and trunk of a tree in a violent storm. But the self-concerned roots remain below the surface. And out of those roots a new negative emotion grows—that's shame.

The gnawing emotion of shame can be a powerful, devastating force in a parent's or a family's life. Not only is it basically a prideful attitude that may be easily translated into envy and jealousy (as Marcie Klein and other parents admitted to me), but it can become a self-destroying emotion that grows by feeding on its own wounds.

One respected educator-counselor I talked with described shame as a vicious cycle. "Something can be done about guilt, a wrong committed," he said. "But people suffering from shame are going round and round in isolation and alienation—with a lack of language to express their true feelings."

A perfect example of this is the story of a widow who was forced to raise her children without a father. When her oldest son got kicked out of her church's denominational college, she withdrew in embarrassment from the fellowship of her Christian friends at church and in her neighborhood.

"But even in hiding, the shame kept growing inside me," she said. "I couldn't reach out for help, and no one on the outside could reach in. I was literally a prisoner behind walls of my own making. I was so bound up in my own feelings I couldn't even see the problems as they really were. I was completely helpless to solve the problem or to let anyone else try to help. My shame was really my pride; I was too much in bondage to say, 'I hurt.'"

This mother's humiliation isolated her from everyone who could or would have tried to help her deal with her family's problem. It focused her hurt and attention inward and prevented her from seeing the real nature of the problem, let alone finding the remedy.

In other cases, parental shame has directly interfered with possible solutions. I recently heard of one wealthy family who made a great pretense of respectability in their community. Their married son went through a messy, painful divorce and caused his parents great embarrassment. His disastrous marriage resulted in such emotional trauma that he committed himself to a state institution for mental and emotional help. His parents saw his decision as the ultimate disgrace for them and the family. So they used their influence to check him out and bring him home. The son tried again and again to find professional help, but each time, his parents snatched him home again to live "as if everything were fine."

The biggest danger in the shame trap, however, is not that humiliation is self-centered, that it isolates a person from help, or even that it may interfere with possible solutions. The greatest damage shame wreaks is on the parent-child relationship.

Humiliation acts as one more wedge between the two parties. If a son senses his father's shame, any guilt, anger, or feeling of alienation can be greatly compounded. In some cases, a parent's obvious humiliation actually serves to reinforce the problem—perhaps even acting as a self-fulfilling prophecy.

The most graphic example of this danger was shared with me by a young woman we'll call Karen. She kept her abortion as a seventeen-year-old a secret for two years, hoping to spare her parents deep hurt.

"But my guilt grew heavier and heavier," Karen said, "until I couldn't carry it alone anymore. I had to tell someone. Just deciding to talk to my folks gave me the first sweet feeling of release I'd felt for months. I knew telling them was going to be the hardest thing I'd ever done. But I was sure they would be relieved to know it was over and I was willing to confess to them.

"I wanted to break the news gently. But there was no way. So I just blurted it out and tried to explain. The blow was too much for my parents to handle. The whole sky fell in on our little living room confession scene. They were so shocked they didn't even try to comprehend my feelings.

"My mother acted the martyr. She spent the next two days hiding in her bedroom. The third day when our paths crossed in the hallway, she exploded. She called me a whore. 'I can't even stand to look at you,' she muttered as she fled back to her room and slammed the door.

"I was crushed. Didn't she know I'd suffered enough? I had already felt forsaken by God. I couldn't live with my own guilt. And now my own mother couldn't even stand to face me. I had worked up my courage to make a confession to the only people I felt could ever understand my feelings and forgive me. But their shame overshadowed everything.

"I didn't think I deserved to be called a whore. *But if that's what they think, the hell with it! I'll be one!* I thought. And from that moment, I hardened my heart, stiffened my neck, and said, 'World, here I come!' I made a determined decision to take a plunge into the depths of sin, and I didn't surface again for years."

Stories such as Karen's, and conversations with people from all walks of life, from all across the country, have confirmed in my mind that shame is one of the most common and dangerous reactions hurting parents experience. The emotion and the isolation it causes must be faced and overcome—and we will look at some additional ways of doing that in the next chapter.

A good place to begin would be to consider a question posed by a Christian college president whose teenage son had been guilty of behavior unbecoming the offspring of such an institutional leader. "I was angrily making my way to my son's room to confront him," this educator said, "when a still, small voice seemed to probe, 'Are you more concerned about your own reputation than you are about your son and his real needs?'"

That is a question every hurting parent must ask himself or herself. Are we more concerned about what others think about us than we are about our own children? Shame says we are.

SOMETHING TO THINK ABOUT

1. What were some of the factors that triggered shame in the parents written about in this chapter? What other factors might prompt a shame reaction?

2. Do you agree or disagree with the statement "Humility and shame are very different, if not opposite"? Explain why and give additional examples.

3. Look again at Karen's story near the end of the chapter. What might her mother have realistically done or said that might have produced a different result?

4. Try to remember a time when you may have been more concerned about what others were thinking about you than you were about your son or daughter. Share that experience if you feel you can.

CHAPTER 3
FELLOWSHIP

Shared joy is doubled; shared sorrow is divided in half.
—Old German proverb

Annie Mueller was a model junior high student and daughter. She made the honor roll every term, won awards as a debater, took leadership in numerous school and church functions, and wholeheartedly engaged in any and every family activity. Her parents had reason to feel proud.

But within months of the time Annie started high school, everything changed. She began bucking authority at school and at home. She joined the staff of a radical underground newspaper that school officials had banned. Her grades dropped. She skipped church unless she was forced to go. She grew surly and uncooperative at home.

As the months of uneasy coexistence passed, Annie's lines of communication with her family withered from lack of use. Annie became a stranger to her parents, especially to her father, Eric Mueller, who was a family counselor by profession. For some reason that Eric couldn't understand, his little girl had suffered a terrible Jekyll-and-Hyde transformation.

Annie got caught smoking pot in her father's car, parked in front of her school. Eric suspected his daughter was experimenting with other drugs, and he was frustrated with his own inability to deal with the situation. But he wasn't genuinely worried until he found the letter.

He found it lying open on the living room coffee table. Eric didn't even know whose letter it was until he read the salutation, "Dear Annie," and discovered the writer was Cam Monroe, the son of a local minister friend. Eric knew Cam had been on drugs during high school, but he had gotten straightened out and was attending college several hundred miles away.

For three handwritten pages Cam lectured Annie on the danger of drugs. The convincing arguments encouraged Eric as he began to read. But by the time Eric reached the end of the letter he realized Cam's warnings were a direct response to a previous letter from Annie — a letter in which Annie had evidently tried to impress Cam with stories of her drug experiences. As the realization of his daughter's involvement began to sink in, so did a soul-wrenching fear.

In the midst of his emotions, Eric felt a sense of gratitude toward Cam Monroe. Cam represented hope — a single voice of sanity to which Annie might listen. Eric decided to call Pastor Monroe and thank him for his son's letter and concern. *Besides*, he thought, *I need someone to talk to who can understand what I'm going through — someone who has felt what I feel.* But it didn't work.

Rev. Monroe answered his phone, and the two exchanged greetings. When Eric started telling about the letter, Eric could feel his friend go cold — even over the telephone lines. The minister hadn't realized Eric had known about Cam's drug trouble, and he was obviously too embarrassed to discuss the subject. He cut off the conversation, made a couple of awkward comments about an unrelated topic, and bade a strained and hasty good-bye. Eric was left holding a dead phone with not so much as a word of encouragement or understanding.

In the following days and weeks, the atmosphere in the Mueller house worsened. Communication between Annie and her dad deteriorated to nothing outside of an occasional confrontation and shouting match. Annie finally announced she was leaving home to move in with some high school roommates. During the argument that ensued, Annie paused and asked accusingly, "You don't like me anymore, do you?"

Eric glared at his daughter and answered, "You're right. I don't like you. I hate you for what you're doing to your mother and me."

Annie smiled a little sadly. "Dad," she said, "when you say you hate me, at least you're being honest. And I appreciate that." Those words ripped into Eric's heart. He turned and walked from the room. What more could he say? He had told his own daughter he hated her, and she had thanked him for being honest. He knew he didn't really hate Annie, but for an instant he had meant what he had said. Eric retreated to his study, closed the door, and sank to his chair in utter defeat.

"For years as a counselor I had unemotionally dealt with the problems of other people, other families," he said. "I couldn't take the realization that I had failed as a father."

Eric finally emerged from his study a discouraged, beaten man. "I'll never speak on families again," he told his wife as they prepared for bed. "If a family counselor can't deal with his own family, he doesn't have anything worth telling others."

Ten minutes after Eric made that pronouncement, at eleven o'clock at night, the phone rang. The pastor of a large church in an East Coast city asked Eric if he would be able to speak at an interdenominational conference his church planned to sponsor. Instinctively Eric accepted the invitation. The pastor promised to write more details, and the conversation was over before Eric realized he had broken his new vow.

In the weeks before the conference, Annie moved out. And Eric vowed anew that this would be his last address as a family expert.

The first day of the conference went smoothly. Eric spoke twice on the subject "What Is Love?" But on the second day, Annie kept invading his thoughts. When the leader of the afternoon session announced a quiet time of prayer and meditation "to just let the Lord lead," Eric couldn't keep Annie out of his mind. As he sat in that giant sanctuary with two thousand silent conferees, he began to feel a prodding, "Get up and tell these people about your problems with your daughter." The longer he sat, the surer Eric felt that God wanted him to share his hurt.

But I can't do that, he told himself. *What'll they think if they know the truth? Everything I've said at this conference will go right down the drain.*

Finally, reluctantly, Eric gave in to that growing inner pressure. He stood, faced the crowd, and began to speak. He had no idea what he was going to say when he started—but the words just came. He told of the breakdown in communication with his daughter. He confessed he had no answers. And he admitted his frustration, his discouragement, and his hurt.

When Eric sat down, another man stood up to address the group. Then another and another. For the next three hours broken people stood to admit honestly their problems and their needs. Dozens of parents like Eric rose to confess their own and their families' hurts. Men in high denominational positions admitted they had always tried to project a self-sufficient, together image, then told of long-hidden family heartaches and asked for the group's prayers.

"That afternoon session was the turning point of the conference," Eric said. "It became a sharing, supporting fellowship of needy Christian brothers and sisters. In fact, I still have a close, open fellowship with a number of those people.

"My own confession at that conference marked a turning point in my problem with Annie. Once I opened my hurt to others, I no longer felt I had anything to hide. My frustration and shame dissolved; I felt liberated. For the first time I was able to reach out in acceptance and love to Annie and her problems. When she finally called a few weeks later, I told her I would come and get her. She agreed to come home, and we began to rebuild our family."

Eric Mueller's feeling of helpless aloneness, like the shame-forced isolation referred to in the preceding chapter, is symptomatic of one of the biggest and yet most common problems hurting parents have shared with me. That problem is a lack of meaningful, supportive fellowship.

Again and again as I have interviewed and shared with parents, I have heard them lament, "I was just so alone," or "There was no one to talk to," or "I didn't know a single person who could understand." Like shipwrecked survivors stranded alone on some remote South Seas island, they yearn for some sort of human contact and comfort. But they are afraid to start swimming for help because they don't even know in which direction to head.

Tragically, many shamed, hurting parents go for years without finding any fellowship. But the stories like Eric's, plus personal experience with my own hurts, have convinced me of the importance and benefits of open, supportive relationships with like-minded people.

One of the strongest witnesses to the value of fellowship was a close friend, Clarice. For the past four years, she, another friend, and I have met for a weekly hour of sharing and prayer. Not long ago she tried to express what our fellowship had meant to her.

"Shame and despair over my rebellious children had nearly swallowed me up for years," she admitted. "But meeting and sharing in prayer and Bible study helped pull me out of myself.

"I can't measure the impact of our fellowship in my life. I live for our Thursday afternoon sessions. Our time has done more for me than therapy could have accomplished. Psychiatrists may have helped me bare my soul, but my soul has never been left bare with you friends. Your words and God's Word have become my strength. Your prayers have helped carry my burdens.

"I don't think it's humanly possible to cope alone with a son who's on court probation and methadone treatment for heroin addiction. Without your support and concern, without your willingness and ability to feel with me, I would have had a nervous breakdown. Our fellowship has been my only survival."

I recently had a chance to visit three women in another state who also meet on a weekly basis for the same kind of fellowship. Barb and her husband are agonizing over a beautiful daughter, an excellent student at a state university who is devoting her social interests to one nonindustrious fellow with little apparent ability and no spiritual interests.

Judy is watching her daughter's marriage coming apart at the seams. And Melissa's doctor son has told his folks their faith is fine for them, but he just can't believe in God anymore.

All three of these mothers value their weekly sharing times. Melissa explained, "Somehow we don't think so much about our own children. Our time together prevents us from getting bogged down in our own circumstances. If something good happens with one of us during the week, the other two feel encouraged. Without this mutual support, our lives would be pretty heavy."

Melissa and Clarice both hinted at one of the strongest benefits of open fellowship. It helps pull a hurting parent outside of himself or herself. It focuses some concern on other people's problems, and sharing gets the problem out of the hidden recesses of the mind and heart into the open where it can be better understood.

Encouragement is another obvious benefit of meaningful fellowship. We can be weighted down and discouraged by the circumstances looming around us, but other people are more objective. Sometimes they can point out progress and bright spots we are too close to notice. They can help pinpoint the problems in our reactions and even lift low moods into more optimistic feelings.

When my son Mark took off unannounced, I was worried sick because we didn't receive any mail. I just knew he must have wrecked his motorcycle in a ditch somewhere. But another mother who had gone through similar experiences with her son told me, "Don't expect to get any mail. Boys don't think like we do." Her words didn't really cheer me, but her objectivity gave me a measure of understanding I desperately needed.

Words of insight, encouragement, and even helpful advice can be valuable by-products of fellowship. They certainly can't occur without a spirit of open honesty and a desire for sharing with others.

But you don't have to receive advice to reap benefits from sharing. I think of a woman who stopped by my house a couple of years ago. She'd read an earlier edition of *The Hurting Parent*. And since we had been acquainted years before when she'd lived in our town, she paid me a visit. She told me about her Christian daughter who had recently gotten married because she was expecting. This distressed mother filled me in about her sad story and admitted she'd been physically sick with worry since she learned about the pregnancy and the young couple's hasty plans for a wedding. "I know I can't go on like this," she said, "or this is going to destroy my health. But I don't know what to do." She went on to talk about her sense of disappointment and the shattering of so many dreams her daughter had had and that she'd had for her daughter. She talked for two hours. And when it came time for her to leave, she said, "I can't tell you how much talking with you has helped. I feel better than I have felt in months."

And yet I had said almost nothing; I had just let her talk. She felt better not because of any advice she'd gotten from me. She felt better solely because she had opened up and shared her deepest hurt with someone she knew understood a little of that hurt.

If the benefits are so great, why isn't there more fellowship among hurting parents? And if the hurting-parent problem is as widespread as I have found it to be, why do some parents feel they are all alone suffering with a problem no one else could possibly understand? I think there are a number of explanations.

Perhaps the most common obstacle to the breaking out of our private shame is fear of emotional hurt. We naturally want to protect ourselves, to avoid vulnerability. Like Eric Mueller who argued with himself, "What will they think of me?" many of us try to hide our crises with our children because we dread the judgment of others. We are afraid of being viewed as failures.

A good example of this was shared with me by a hurting grandfather. (Grandparents share many of the same hurts and concerns over their grandchildren as parents do. And we've heard from a number of them since the first edition of this book.) "When we learned to our dismay that our college grandson had gotten mixed up with drugs and was in legal trouble," he recounted, "my wife's first reaction was 'Oh, dear! Let's not tell anyone about this!' But my reaction was just the opposite. I said, 'We must tell our friends so they can be praying with us about this.' Not long after that I came in contact with one of the bishops of my denomination. We'd been acquainted for years, and when he asked about my family, I told him about my grandson. He listened compassionately and promised to pray with us about the situation. We've felt a lot of strength and support from the prayers of friends who wouldn't have known to pray if we hadn't shared with them."

Our strong cultural attitudes of independence and self-sufficiency also prohibit the seeking of fellowship. The kind of pride talked about in the preceding chapter influences this reluctance. We want to deal with our own problems in our own way. Or we just ignore or repress our feelings so we don't have to admit to anyone, including ourselves, that we need help.

Fellowship means risks. Honesty makes us vulnerable. Some parents have told me they finally worked up the courage to admit their hurts only to be rebuffed. Eric Mueller experienced that when he called his minister friend. Another parent, a middle-aged mother named Clara, shared her experience. "I was deeply troubled about the roommates my twenty-year-old son was living with," she told me. "One day at work on my break time I opened up and shared just a bit of my fears about my son. My Christian employer told me not to bring my personal problems to work. I can't describe the blow I felt. Months of bottled-up pain followed. But finally God gave me courage to admit to a friend, 'I hurt.' And with her I found encouragement and support."

Parents like Clara have to overcome intensified fear of hurt and vulnerability before they can reach out for help and comfort again. Some never do.

Every hurting parent needs to be aware of a few cautions. Some friends might not be able to continue to accept your son or daughter if they know your worries and concerns; you want to be careful not to risk damaging your child's relationship with others. The people you share with need to be discreet. It could greatly damage your relationship if your child thought you had exposed the nitty-gritty details of his or her life to the general public. (I should probably add here that I shared my own experience with my son Mark only after I showed him what I'd written in this manuscript and had received his permission to use it.)

Another consideration is that some people shouldn't be fellowshiping together; they react to and feed on each other's suffering and discouragement. They only multiply each other's misery.

Perhaps the best gauge of helpful fellowship is the list of benefits discussed in the preceding pages. If you have been sharing your hurts with someone and you are not seeing at least some of those pluses, you aren't getting meaningful, positive fellowship. If that's the case, you need to start looking elsewhere for the supportive fellowship you need.

Where do you find people willing to share and care with you? True and meaningful fellowship for hurting parents needs to start at home. But often it doesn't. I have known hurting wives and husbands who have been unwilling to open up and share their worries and concerns about their children with each other. Even to themselves they have not wanted to expose their hurt. It is as if they think they can deny the problems by not voicing them.

Yet most of the benefits of fellowship we have mentioned can result from honest sharing between husband and wife. One mother whose son was in and out of trouble from the time he was ten years old until his early twenties said, "I would have sunk into despair without my husband. He constantly reminded me we dare not dwell on our own hurt. We needed to try to understand our son and his problems."

Many hurting parents have testified to the strength and encouragement gained from spouses. But there are of course valuable advantages to additional fellowship with other parents. For example, husband-wife fellowship can't possibly offer the objectivity another couple could bring to a time of sharing. And when a hurting parent is single, or his or her spouse isn't Christian, that person especially needs the support and fellowship of other hurting parents.

If you are a hurting parent, think of the people you know in your community or church who have been hurting parents. Take the risk of opening up a little to them about your concerns for your children. If they respond in a caring way, you could share a little more and perhaps gradually develop fellowship with them. If they back off, seek your fellowship from someone else.

An even better strategy than this trial-and-error method of finding fellowship would be to go to a pastor or a counselor who might suggest other hurting parents you could talk to. Some counselors make such referrals a general practice.

Jay Kessler, lifelong youth worker, radio counselor, and former president of Taylor University, told me, "When a husband and wife come to me with problems concerning their children, I often contact another couple who have faced similar struggles. Then I arrange for both couples to get together. Time after time great good has come out of that kind of fellowship."

Correspondence can be another effective means of fellowship. An experience I had a few years ago is a strong reminder to me. A friend I had known for twenty years wrote me to tell of her dread of the coming Christmas season. Alice's son Allen was coming home from school for the holidays, and he was bringing his girlfriend who had no Christian sensitivity whatsoever. Alice wrote, "I don't think I can stand to listen to her language again. Last time she was here it was awful."

Almost a month passed before I felt an urgency to answer Alice's letter. I tried to write a note of encouragement, but I don't remember exactly what I said. It certainly wasn't much—just a brief note.

But the next time I saw Alice, months later, she thanked me profusely for the letter. "It came at such a crucial time. I was near physical exhaustion from worry and home from work that day. When I'd psyched up enough energy to go out to the mailbox, I found your letter. I tore it open right there, and as I read it walking back to the house, tears of joy and gratitude streamed down my face. God spoke to me through your admonition: 'You can merely love and accept Allen and his girlfriend where they are; only God can change them.' You'll never know how those words helped me through that Christmas season and the months that have passed since. I praise God for the fellowship you and I have."

All I did was write a note of encouragement. But because Alice and I had been willing to honestly share with each other—both in person and by letter—we had established a spirit of fellowship that has strengthened us both.

Churches also should be an open-armed source of fellowship, strength, and support for all kinds of hurting people. Sometimes congregations fail at these tasks, but those churches that do fulfill their divinely appointed tasks of caring can have a powerful impact on the lives of hurting parents and their children.

I think of friends whose son gave up the faith he was taught as a child and decided to marry a Jewish girl. The parents anguished over their son's decisions. But when the time came for the wedding, a dozen people from their small church flew hundreds of miles with the family to attend the ceremony. These fellow church members knew the hurt my friends were suffering and wanted to lend their support. Think what their caring said to these parents, to their son, and to the Jewish family of the bride.

The Bible emphasizes this style of caring fellowship. Paul directed the Galatian church to "help carry one another's burdens, and in this way you will obey the law of Christ" (Gal. 6:2 TEV).

The Hebrew Christians were exhorted, "Let us be concerned for one another, to help one another to show love and to do good. Let us not give up the habit of meeting together, as some are doing. Instead, let us encourage one another all the more" (Heb. 10:24–25 TEV). Such fellowship is the natural outgrowth of Christ's teaching and an example of love for God and love for neighbors—the "law of Christ" to which Paul referred.

The fellowship that hurting parents need has a price: a certain vulnerability and a risk of emotional hurt. And it costs unselfishness—a willingness to care about others and their problems. But most of all, fellowship demands openness and honesty—with yourself, with others, and with God.

The price is high. But every hurting parent I have ever talked to who has found and given supportive fellowship has said it is worth the risks. The eminent psychologist counselor Carl Rogers, in his book *On Becoming a Person*, seconded this conclusion. He said, "To discover that it is not devastating to accept the positive feelings from another, that it does not necessarily end in hurt, that it actually 'feels good' to have another person with you in your struggles to meet life—this may be one of the most profound learnings encountered by the individual whether in therapy or not."

For some hurting parents I have known, that "profound learning" on the value of fellowship has been the deciding factor in their emotional and spiritual survival.

SOMETHING TO THINK ABOUT

1. What are some of the benefits of fellowship for the hurting parents referred to in this chapter? What other possible benefits or examples can you think of?

2. Use a concordance or a topical Bible and summarize what God's Word has to say about the value of fellowship. What passages about fellowship seem most relevant?

3. Brainstorm creative ways you might minister to some hurting parent you know. What could a church do to minister to this group of people? What could the Christian community as a whole do?

4. If you're a hurting parent, consider honestly sharing your hurt right now (or in the coming week) with another person you suspect is a hurting parent. If you're not a hurting parent, pray for someone else who is.

CHAPTER 4

REJECTION

There exists no cure for a heart wounded
with the sword of separation.
—Hitopadesa

Next case," intoned the judge. The bailiff opened the door to the hall and announced in a loud voice, "Harper." A handful of adults filed into the empty juvenile court. A door on the side of the courtroom opened, and a uniformed deputy escorted a teenage boy into the room.

Quickly and silently the principals found their positions. They had all been through this before. Seventeen-year-old Jerry Harper stood directly in front of the judge wearing a standard prison uniform — a simple, pocketless T-shirt, black pants, and tennis shoes. With his head hung low, his shoulder-length hair fell forward over the sides of his face, partially hiding his tear-reddened eyes. Next to him, on his left, stood his attorney.

Several feet to Jerry's right were his parents, Howard and Ellen Harper. Howard, a ruggedly built construction contractor, stood at rigid attention — his hands clasped behind his arrow-straight back, his eyes fixed on the judge, his lips pursed. Ellen Harper, a small, pale woman, stood next to her husband, wringing a handkerchief in her hands. This was the fourth time her son had appeared before this same judge — each time for a different offense.

Just to the right of Ellen Harper was the state's attorney, and to his right the probation officer. The clerk and the bailiff were the only others present in the court. The judge surveyed the entire group as a clerk handed him a legal folder and said, "Jerome Harper."

The judge opened the folder and spread the papers in front of him. "What's the charge?" he asked without looking up.

The state's attorney stood and began to read. After two brief paragraphs of legalese, he got to the final crucial lines: "Jerome Harper is charged with illegal possession of a controlled substance."

The judge frowned down at Jerry and delivered a well-practiced line. "Young man," he said, "there's something you need to learn before it's too late: Losers use pot and pot uses losers." That said, the judge paused to watch Jerry's nonreaction before he asked, "How do you plead?"

The defense attorney answered, "My client pleads guilty, Your Honor."

The judge made no response except to ask the probation officer for his workup, a short report of the facts and circumstances. The officer read the three-page report and concluded by saying, "Your Honor, we recommend Jerome Harper be taken out of his home environment."

The judge studied the papers in the folder in front of him for a moment. Then he looked down at the parents and asked, "Mr. and Mrs. Harper, what do you want done with your son?"

"I think jail's the place for him, Your Honor," Howard Harper said. "He's got to learn his lesson sometime before—"

"Not jail!" Ellen Harper cried out. "Put him in a foster home or maybe even the county youth home. But not jail."

"Quit trying to protect him, Ellen," Mr. Harper answered. "He's got to learn—"

"I think you should put him in the youth home, Your Honor," Ellen Harper interrupted. "We can't do anything with him anymore, that's for cer—"

Howard Harper interrupted his wife again, and they began the argument all over again. The scene was too much for Jerry Harper. He burst into tears. "Send me away!" he screamed. "I can't stand to live with them, and they don't want me. I don't care where. Just send me away!"

The judge pounded his gavel and shouted for quiet. Mr. and Mrs. Harper fell silent. Jerry shook with soundless sobs.

The judge quickly shuffled his papers and addressed the parents. "I seriously recommend that you two continue seeking the help of a counselor. As for Jerome Harper, I'm sentencing him to a term of one to two years in the county's youth correctional facility." Just that suddenly, the hearing was over. A tearful Ellen Harper tried to talk to her son. But Jerry turned quickly and walked out of the room escorted by his guard.

The court-appointed counselor who had been responsible for providing family therapy for the Harpers told me their story, without revealing their real names, of course. He said these Christian parents generally wanted what was best for their son. The father knew he couldn't control his son; he was convinced hard punishment would help. Although Mrs. Harper didn't want the drastic action her husband did, she too wanted to turn her son over to someone else for help.

Jerry was naturally bitter at his parents' rejection. In time, some of that bitterness began to ease. But it was replaced by an intense feeling of self-condemnation. "He took on the guilt of the whole family," said the counselor. "He not only blamed himself for his own troubles, but for his parents' marital problems as well."

A number of years ago, newspapers across the country picked up the story of John, a young boy who waited in an idling car while a group of his friends burglarized a small business in a Midwestern city. What gave the story an unusual twist was that the store belonged to the boy's father. But even more surprising than that was the reaction of the boy's father when the son was apprehended.

When the guilt of the boy was verified, the family retaliated by announcing their son had died. Then they held official funeral services, which were attended by family and friends. From that day on, for his relatives, John ceased to exist.

Edna and Barney Snyder sent their daughter Paula to a Christian college to get "some good training." But late one night during her sophomore year, she sneaked off campus and hitchhiked to a neighboring town for a little excitement.

The only place open was a bar, so she went in. A twenty-five-year-old divorced man spotted her and quickly made her acquaintance. She soon melted under his attention.

Together they wrote seven hundred dollars' worth of cold checks and skipped the state. A thousand miles away and ten days later, Paula came to her senses. Embarrassed and regretful, she returned to face her deeds.

The courts released her to her father for an eighteen-month suspended sentence. But her mother refused to have anything to do with her. Edna had already held a burial service; she also had burned and buried all of Paula's clothes and refused to speak to her.

A few years ago I found an Associated Press news report out of Florida. The story began: "After two years of trying to get rid of the adopted son they considered a troublemaker, a [name of city] couple has persuaded a judge to cancel the adoption." The fifteen-year-old boy had been arrested after admitting he had taken part in a burglary of his adopted parents' home.

The father said, "We've been actively trying to get rid of him for two years." The couple, fundamentalist Christians, had adopted the boy when he was ten and had frequent problems with him, such as running away, poor grades, and fighting.

The court temporarily assigned the boy to a county group home to await possible readoption, placement in a foster home, or permanent assignment to a group home. The adoptive parents were required to contribute reasonable financial support until he could be permanently placed. And the judge who ruled in the case said, "In a situation like this, no one ever wins. There's a lot of forgiving to do. A lot of rebuilding to do."

Webster says that *reject* means "to cast off" or "to spew out." That is certainly the kind of rejection illustrated by the parents in the preceding cases. Of course, these examples are extreme; premature funerals and revoked adoptions are not the norm.

Most of the hurting parents I have talked to would say, "I could never bring myself to do that." The idea of rejection is just too abhorrent. And yet I have come to the conclusion that a lot of hurting parents practice a subtler form of rejection.

"To refuse to accept or consider" is another dictionary definition of *reject*. So while we usually think of rejection as a determined action, an active cutting-off, it can take a passive form. In other words, rejection can also occur when a parent withdraws from or withholds something from his or her relationship with a child. And most of us are guilty of this, at least occasionally.

A withholding of communication is one of the most common ways it happens. The case in chapter 2 of the girl who told her parents about her abortion is a good example. Instead of talking about the problem, the mother retreated to her room and refused to communicate for days.

Yet the circumstances need not be so extreme. Take the case of the college-age girl who was dating a non-Christian. An argument ensued every time her concerned Christian parents questioned the wisdom of the arrangement. The girl always insisted she was old enough to make her own decisions and lead her own life. Her parents knew they couldn't govern her life when she was away at school. They were frustrated and worried. Whenever the daughter made it home for a weekend, an uneasy feeling of truce prevailed. So to avoid further fights they feared would only serve to solidify their daughter's feelings, the parents steered clear of any discussion of college. When the girl was home, her parents kept conversation limited to safe subjects, such as current events, family, and hometown friends. What resulted was an unnatural withholding of communication about a major area of the daughter's life. As such, it was a form of limited rejection.

Passive rejection can also result when a parent withholds affirmation or encouragement from a child. A son made excellent grades all through school. Every time he brought home his report card, his parents had commended him—despite the fact they had come to expect high marks. His senior year in high school, the boy shocked his parents when he was arrested for possession of marijuana. Two weeks later he brought home another exemplary report card, but his parents still felt such keen disappointment that they just signed it without any positive comment. Any such withholding of deserved praise, especially if a child has come to expect it, can be a form of rejection.

The same can be said for the withholding of emotional support, involvement, and interest in a child's life. For example, a girl who grew up as an active participant in her father-pastor's church decided to do her graduate work in geology. Halfway through her studies she confronted her folks with her feelings that what her professors of science were telling her didn't jibe with her parents' beliefs; consequently, she said she couldn't believe in her parents' God anymore.

Her mother and father were so devastated by her admission that when she graduated with honors from her graduate program a few months later, they couldn't even bring themselves to attend.

This withholding of something from a relationship or the refusal to accept or consider is widely practiced by hurting Christian parents. Curiously, the rationales and the explanations are the same for this passive rejection as for the cutting-off or kicking-out styles more often associated with the idea of parental rejection.

One of the most common defenses I have heard is this one: "I just couldn't condone what my son [or daughter] was doing." One mother who exemplified this feeling told me about her neighbors who violently opposed long hair on boys. "So when we were with these friends," she said, "I would take repeated advantage of the opportunity to publicly remind my sixteen-year-old son that I had given him haircut money two weeks earlier. Or I'd make some other equally obvious comment to make sure my friends understood my position." By making such a point of withholding her acceptance, this mother was publicly rejecting her son.

This "seeming to condone" argument can't hold water. Teenage and young adult children know what their parents approve and believe. If they don't, they are in need of education, not rejection. And if Christian parents choose to reject a son or daughter because they don't want neighbors or church members thinking they condone certain behavior, they need to consider again the question raised at the end of the chapter on shame: "Are we more concerned with what others think about us than we are about our own children?"

Rejection can be a form of retaliation for hurt or humiliation. Christian parents are human; sometimes when we feel deeply wounded and rejected ourselves, we may instinctively strike back with rejection and feel justified in doing so. One father said, "Our youngest son, Art, brought shame on our family name and my professional reputation for years. When he was finally convicted of murdering his business partner, I refused to visit him in prison. I didn't want anyone in the family to go either."

The threat of rejection is often a desperate attempt at control. "As long as you live under my roof, you'll live by my rules," is a common ultimatum. "When you cross my lines, you're out." And those lines can be drawn in any of a million places, depending on the experience and standards of a parent.

I have known of parents who kicked their teenage daughter out of the house when they learned she was pregnant and others who disinherited a son when he married a non-Christian girl. I have heard of boys banished from home because of the length or style of their hair and even one case back in the '60s of a father running out his son when the boy defied his wishes and bought a pair of wire-rimmed "granny" glasses.

And then there was the case of the high school senior who was kicked out the door when his staunchly Republican parents learned he had just registered to vote as a Democrat. Only through the appeal of the family's pastor was the boy allowed to return home and live for the remaining few months until he left home for college. That "boy" grew up, began raising a fine Christian family, and became so successful in his profession that he was appointed to a high government position in Washington (in a Democratic administration). But even now, according to the family member who told me the story, almost thirty years later there remains a strain in the family over that incident.

And since we published the first edition of *The Hurting Parent*, I have heard numerous other rejection stories. A few parents have written to describe the "firm" steps they have taken with their children and to ask my opinion. More often I have heard the stories from family members who are having to live with the repercussions of parental rejection. One young woman wrote to tell me how her adult sister, who lives with a man she has never married, is not allowed through the door of her parents' home if her father is there. Another young woman wrote to tell me about her sister-in-law whose radical feminism so offended her conservative Christian father that no one in the family was allowed to mention her name in his presence.

Now, there may be some examples of parental rejection effectively shaking up and turning around a son or daughter, but I haven't heard any. The testimonies of the people I have talked to in researching this book have convinced me that rejection is a dangerous strategy of either control or punishment. Even unthinking, passive forms of rejection can open deep, painful wounds that can result in bitterness, hatred, and regret.

The impact of rejection was illustrated in the case of Will, a young army social worker who told his Christian parents he was going to marry his fiancée with or without their approval. "I knew they weren't happy," he said, "but the letter I got from my mom was a complete shock. She said, 'Don't bother calling home. As far as we're concerned, you were killed in Vietnam.'

"Of course I tried to call. But the moment my folks heard my voice, the phone would click and I would be cut off. I wrote letter after letter, but they weren't answered. I was a pretty strong person with training in psychology and counseling. But this rejection devastated me emotionally. After five months of isolation from my family, I felt dead.

"Eventually we reestablished contact. But I can't feel my parents love me anymore. After fourteen years now, that old rejection still affects every contact I have with my parents. And it will be an emotional handicap the rest of my life. I can't box it up and forget it. The memory is there in the back of my mind all the time."

Parents, too, can suffer in the aftermath of their rejection of their children. A visiting speaker had just concluded a luncheon address about the needs of youth to a civic club in an eastern Canadian city when a big, burly man stepped in front of him and shook his hand.

"I want to show you something," he said to the speaker, pulling out his wallet and pushing aside a couple of plates to clear a place on the table. Carefully, one at a time, this man took five well-worn photos of young men from his billfold and placed them side by side. "Those five boys are my sons," he said, his voice catching. "And I drove every one of them out of my home!"

He went on to say that he had been a military man all his life. Discipline was his lifestyle. And as a Christian father, he expected obedience from his sons. He laid down the rules, and if they didn't like them, they were free to leave. All five boys had left home after high school. "And I haven't seen one of them since," the man said.

Again he reached into his billfold. This time he pulled out a picture of a grinning ten-year-old boy and put it down beside the other five. "That's my youngest. He's the only one I have left. I swear to God I'm not going to make the same mistake with him."

This father was a broken, remorseful man. He had resorted to rejection as a last-ditch effort to control his sons, and he had failed. He felt guilty and confused because his actions had been well intentioned; his strategy had been prompted by his own deep fears for his children and genuine feelings of loving concern.

The ironic and seemingly contradictory idea that rejection may be a justifiable and even necessary expression of a Christian parent's loving concern is a startlingly common feeling, especially among more conservative and fundamentalist believers. A few years ago, I saw a tract written in the form of a letter from a "concerned" Christian parent to his son. You can probably guess the date of origin from the issues the tract addressed. It railed against everything from long hair, peace symbols, and rock music fans to the National Council of Churches, peace protesters, and communism. It concluded with this threat: "My son, I love you dearly. I have done and will continue to do all I can for your good in every way. But if you should ever decide to turn away from God, Country, and everything decent by joining this group of scum who burn our American flag, then burn your birth certificate as well. From that day on, you will cease to be a son of mine. — Your very devoted Father."

Somehow people like this father and the ex-military man who drove five sons out of his home have come to feel it is their Christian obligation to force their children to toe a strict line or else. And often they seem to feel their ideas are supported and encouraged by their Christian friends and their churches.

If that is true, our churches are badly mistaken. We ought to give more consideration to God's example. Even with all his power, he didn't try to coerce his children into doing his will. In fact, if we carefully study the nature of God and scriptural families, we discover that the overwhelming emphasis for parents is not control or punishment, but love.

Perhaps some of this "shape up or ship out" attitude is a misapplication of the "tough love" and "intervention" principles advocated by some counselors and by groups who work with chemically dependent people who need to be forced to face the consequences of their problems. And there is no doubt a place for "tough love" in some situations. But there is a big difference between rejection and "tough" (or any other kind of) love.

Rejection, in fact, is the opposite of love. By its very nature it is a denial of further responsibility and concern. Rejection is the ultimate expression of defeat. But there is another argument against rejection: it solidifies positions. It seldom does anything to reconcile differences. It more often increases them.

Every hurting Christian parent feels a barrier, a wall of misunderstanding and disagreement between himself and his child. But that barrier is often of the child's construction. Rejection, on the other hand, is a parentally constructed barrier that serves to reinforce the already existing wall. And sometimes the resulting double wall is almost impossible to knock down.

Rejection is a powerful force, but its power is negative. Rejection tears apart, reinforces walls, separates, and wounds. However, there is another, even more powerful force—a positive force that draws together, unifies, knocks down barriers, and heals wounds. We will examine this positive power in the lives and experiences of the hurting parents who share in the next chapter.

SOMETHING TO THINK ABOUT

1. How would you define *passive rejection*?

2. What are you most tempted to withhold when you have been hurt or upset by one of your children?

3. What arguments might someone give for rejecting a rebellious child?

4. What arguments could be used against rejection?

CHAPTER 5

ACCEPTANCE

Only the reassurance of an accepting and understanding love
will lure the anxious, the guilt-ridden, and the supposedly
inferior persons out from behind their defenses.
—John Powell, S.J.

"Follow me," said the young man as Bruce and Millie Crane handed him their tickets. Silently he led them down the long aisle of the still empty auditorium. He didn't stop until he reached the second row in front of the stage. "Here you are," he said as he turned around. "Best seats in the house. Hope you enjoy the performance."

"I expect we will," Millie responded. "Our daughter is in the play." The usher smiled in response and retreated back up the aisle as the Cranes settled into their special reserved seats to wait. It had been nearly a month since their daughter Andrea had called long distance from Boston to excitedly announce that she had won a big dramatic role in her community theater and to invite them to come for this performance.

"Of course we'll come, honey," Bruce Crane had assured her. "We wouldn't miss it."

The eight-hour drive to Boston didn't matter. Bruce and Millie were anxious to capitalize on any and every opportunity to show their acceptance and affirmation to Andrea and her husband, Ed. The Crane's telephone bill usually took the brunt of their concern. Every month they placed or accepted countless long-distance calls to and from Andrea. But Bruce and Millie willingly paid that price to keep communication lines open.

There hadn't always been such need for concern. When Bruce, a hospital chaplain, had performed the marriage for Andrea and Ed, they had been a committed Christian couple just out of college and excited about their futures. But after they had moved to Boston for Ed's graduate work, their faith had been eroded slowly by their academic and social environments. They gradually drifted away from the church and Christian fellowship until antagonism for Christianity and things Christian began to fill the vacuum left by their fading faith.

Over a period of three years, Bruce and Millie had watched Andrea cast off the values they had always taught. They learned she had begun smoking and drinking. They suspected her experimentation with other drugs. They didn't have to suspect her marital troubles; the growing strain between Andrea and Ed was obvious.

Though they anguished over their daughter and son-in-law, the Cranes kept a close check on their own feelings. "We didn't say a word about the things we observed," explained Bruce. "We didn't feel we had to. Andrea and Ed knew where we stood. Millie and I felt it was much more important to maintain communication and contact by showing our love and acceptance of Andrea and Ed."

But that acceptance sometimes came hard, as it did when the Cranes reached Boston the day before Andrea's play. "From the minute we arrived, we were shocked by her toughness," Millie said. "Her hardness hit us like ice water in our faces. She smoked right in front of us as she spewed tough and vulgar talk. She wore her callousness proudly, like a new dress, as if to say, 'Daddy and Mother, look at me.'"

The impact of their daughter's newly acquired bitterness weighed heavily on Bruce and Millie Crane as they sat and waited for the performance to begin. Finally, the curtain parted and the play began. Only a few minutes of the first scene passed before Andrea made her entrance.

"Despite everything we'd been through with our daughter, we weren't at all prepared for her role," Bruce Crane said. "I can still feel the awful wrenching in my stomach as I watched her traipse onto the stage and parade shamelessly back and forth in her suggestive costume, flaunting herself with bawdy banter. I can still feel Millie squeezing my arm and the lump that rose in my throat when she whispered, 'Oh, Bruce, can this be our sweet little girl?'"

Bruce couldn't bring himself to respond to that question. He only shifted uneasily in his seat and forced himself to endure the rest of the play. "It was one of those risqué English dramas of a century or two ago — a play about life at court where everyone was scheming to sleep with everyone else. I don't remember many details or even the name of the play. In fact, I don't recall much at all about the evening except the feelings churning inside me and the sense of relief that hit me as the final curtain brought an end to the torturous ordeal."

Andrea was occupied backstage after the performance; she had planned to go to the cast party. So Bruce and Millie drove back to their daughter's apartment alone, brimming with mingled emotions. In Millie's words, "We felt angry, disgusted, and heartsick all at the same time."

When morning finally came after a restless night, the Cranes had to face their daughter. They agreed before they went out to the kitchen for breakfast that they wouldn't condemn or criticize.

"But we were tense as we took our seats at the table," Bruce said. "Andrea eagerly poured us hot coffee, seemingly intent to continue her flaunting of the past two days. As she returned to the stove to tend the eggs, she barraged us with questions: How did we like the play? What did we think of her part? What about this scene or the other scene? She kept firing the questions without waiting for our response. By the time the flow of questions stopped, Andrea was serving us the bacon and eggs. As conversation flowed more easily toward food and eating, she stopped trying to get a heated reaction out of us."

During the months that followed, the Cranes's phone bill rose as their daughter's marriage became more and more troubled. Finally, the day came when Andrea called—almost in hysterics. One of her theater friends had tried to rape her. Emotionally devastated, Andrea was on the verge of a breakdown. Ed said he couldn't cope with her anymore.

So Bruce and Millie invited their daughter to stay with them for a few weeks. Andrea seemed so emotionally vulnerable the Cranes did everything they could to encourage and support her. Bruce even footed the bill for some surgery Andrea had been putting off for years.

One night, after an outpouring of despair about her marriage, Andrea retreated to her room. She picked up a bottle of prescribed drugs from the nightstand and threw herself on the bed. As she lay there, seriously contemplating suicide as the only solution to her troubles, she cried out to God.

"Something happened that night," Bruce recalled. "She later told us it was as if Christ came into the room and reentered her life. I know something dramatic happened, because she was a changed woman. A short time later, she went back to Ed and they began to rebuild their lives. Today Andrea and Ed have a Christian family and are actively involved in the ministry of their church in their community.

"As I think back over the struggles and hurts we had with them," said Bruce, "I'd have to say acceptance was the single most important factor through which God chose to work in their lives. If we had rejected them or been critical of the things we saw, Andrea would never have been willing to come home. And I hate to think where she and Ed would have been by now."

Human beings have an unquenchable desire for acceptance. From infancy, children crave assurance of their worth. As much as they need love, they need to feel worthy of love; it is crucial to their self-development and their psychological survival. This basic human need for acceptance is never outgrown. Children of hurting parents are no exception.

One twenty-year-old who recently established his independence by moving away from home adopted a lifestyle marked by regular bouts of drinking and partying. He knew his parents could never approve of actions so different from their Christian standards, but he still needed some sense of parental reassurance. "One day during the holiday season," his mother recalled, "he dropped by the house. And while he was there, he said, 'I didn't get a Christmas card from you and Dad, Mom.' He tried to make his comment sound nonchalant, but I read the tinge of concern in his voice and realized he was feeling for signs of rejection. I quickly tried to explain I didn't send cards to any of our family or friends I knew I'd see in person at Christmas. His only response was a sheepish, 'Well, I sent you one.' So I made a special effort when he was in the hospital for surgery a few weeks later to send him a card and a plant, even though I knew I would visit him at least once each day."

Some appeals for acceptance are even less subtle. I still vividly remember my son Mark's words after I had voiced my disappointment about something he had planned. A definite tone of concern sounded in his voice as he responded, "I hope you can accept me anyway—just the way I am." I tried to assure him I would.

But acceptance isn't always easy to give, as Bruce and Millie Crane would be the first to admit. It takes determined and sometimes painful effort to hold our tongues and our judgments and lovingly accept our children—sins and all.

A number of factors hamper acceptance. One problem we hinted at in the previous chapter is that many hurting Christian parents confuse acceptance with approval. Parents often see acceptance as a negative stance, a surrender of principle, a resigned defeat. That is not the kind of acceptance I'm talking about; it is certainly not the kind of reaction the Cranes felt. Acceptance can be a very positive reaction that distinguishes between a son or daughter who *has* a problem and a son or daughter who *is* a problem. This kind of aggressive acceptance can embrace the person without condoning action or behavior.

It might help to think of acceptance in terms of a related idea that is also the opposite of rejection—reception. We need to receive our children with the same grateful and accepting spirit with which we received them when they came into the world and into our families. Grown-up sons and daughters live lives of their own in ways we might never approve of, but they are still God's gift of life to us as parents. And as with any gift, courtesy and consideration for the Giver demand we graciously receive and accept the gift.

A strong sense of disappointment is one of the most common hindrances to acceptance. As parents we usually have high expectations and dreams for our children. As we rear them and watch them grow, we can't help dreaming of the mark they will someday make for God and maybe even for us and our families. We want them to use every ounce of their potential. When they fail to attain our dreams or they choose some other dreams of their own, we have to struggle with our feelings.

A college professor told of his disappointment with his son, saying, "We had always looked forward to the day when our children would enter college. We remember our own happy college days, and we looked forward to the day when our children could experience college life. We worked and we saved to guarantee them the opportunity.

"But when our oldest son graduated from high school, he announced he wasn't interested in college. We couldn't understand how he could disregard what had meant everything to us. How could he pass up an opportunity we'd worked so hard to provide for him? We were sick at heart over our son's decision, and for a long time we couldn't show much acceptance, I'm afraid. Our disappointment seemed to engulf us."

Concern about what others are thinking and the kind of shame we talked about in chapter 2 undermines acceptance. I think of one couple I was told about whose son underwent a sex-change operation. Imagine their emotions when their "former son" decided to go with them to the next big family reunion. Acceptance wouldn't come easy in a situation such as that.

Fear can also make acceptance difficult. We feel so helpless as we watch our children test the thin ice of independence and the even thinner ice of rebellion. There is a place for experienced advice, and parents are duty-bound to offer it. But when that advice is shunned and we fear the consequences, acceptance comes hard.

It is never easy for hurting parents to acknowledge the independence of someone whose diapers we changed (what seems like) only yesterday. And it is doubly difficult if that son or daughter lives at home or still depends on us for financial support. But no matter the degree of continuing dependence, no matter the understood rules that govern our continuing relationships, there is a growing spirit of independence in every child that demands recognition and respect as a part of acceptance.

That acceptance takes extra effort when a hurting parent feels manipulated or tested. In such cases, little things, minor irritations, and our response to them can be as great a barometer of our acceptance as the major problems and differences.

I recall a visit at a relative's home when an uncle purchased tickets for my husband and sons to go to a Detroit Tiger baseball game. All the men dressed in nice, casual attire to go to the game — except Mark. I couldn't believe my eyes as I looked at his old tacky painter's overalls. *You mean my young adult son is going out in public looking like that?* I thought to myself. *Is this my son who has always had the best taste in clothes since he was a little boy?* I thought of his uncle Howard and how embarrassed he would be. But I was trying hard at that time to be accepting of Mark, so I just bit my tongue and kept silent.

That incident seems a little silly now — merely an insignificant irritation for an overly sensitive mother. But at the time my silence was an acid test of acceptance.

Occasionally, as in this ball game case, silence can be a sign of acceptance. But it is seldom enough.

The kind of acceptance hurting parents need to learn, the kind of acceptance God can use to make an impact on a wayward son or daughter, has to be more than an "I guess I'll have to give in to 'em" resignation from opposition, more than a begrudging tolerance, more even than a positive warm loving feeling we keep bottled up inside.

Any sort of neutral or unexpressed acceptance may be misread as rejection by a child who is especially sensitive to a possible strain in our relationship. (Remember the Christmas card example.)

If, as we said in the preceding chapter, rejection can be the withholding of communication, encouragement, affection, emotional support, interest, and affirmation, then acceptance has to be the opposite. We must strive to maintain or reestablish all these elements in our relationship if we are going to prove our acceptance to our children.

Genuine, aggressive acceptance needs to be expressed in such clear words and acted out in such open-armed fashion that it can't possibly be misunderstood. It must be so obvious, so overwhelming that it sets our children at ease by overcoming the disease that exists because of our differences and because of such feelings as guilt and regret.

The Cranes were a good example of this. Despite their daughter's provocative flaunting and what seemed like deliberate attempts to draw their condemnation, Bruce and Millie Crane welcomed her back into their home and offered her the same kind of loving relationship they had given her all her life.

Another illustration of this kind of unmistakable acceptance was shared with me by a Christian mother whose son is living with his girlfriend. "When Alex came home to tell us he'd moved in with Claudia, I burst into tears, even though I'd halfway expected it for months," Bonnie Ahrens said. "I told him we could never approve, but of course he knew that. I also told him that because he was our son, we would keep loving him no matter what.

"But accepting the girl was impossible as far as I was concerned," Bonnie continued. "I didn't even want to talk to her. But when I expressed my feelings to my own daughter, she said, 'Mom, it's very possible she and Alex will get married someday. And if that happens, I want to like and get along with my sister-in-law.'

"That started me thinking," Bonnie said. "I determined to get my relationship with my son's girlfriend off on the right foot. And I began to look for ways to show my acceptance of her.

"Christmas promised to be an awkward time. But when I learned Alex wanted to bring Claudia over to our house for our family celebration, I decided to make her feel welcome. We spent as much money on gifts for her as we did for our own daughter.

"We had a beautiful Christmas day together as a family. We were all able to relax and enjoy what I had feared might be a strained experience. I know my feelings were accurate, because as Alex and Claudia said their good-byes at the door, Claudia gave my husband an impulsive hug. Then she came to me and gave me a hug.

"As I put my arms around her to squeeze back, my emotions welled up inside me. I didn't want to let go. But when I did and when they were gone, I tried to analyze my feelings. It was as if my deliberate acts of acceptance, the sharing of a Christmas meal, the giving of gifts, had released in me a surge of loving acceptance. For the first time I was really able to care about Claudia.

"Not long after that Claudia said to me, 'Your family is so close. I wish my family could be like that.' Then I knew our attitude of acceptance was making an impression, not only on her, but on our son, Alex."

Acceptance has a way of doing that. Where rejection only creates resistance, acceptance softens, melts, bridges, and soothes. Many other hurting parents I have talked to echo Bruce Crane's feeling that "acceptance has been the single most important factor through which God seemed to work." And a number of hurting parents' sons or daughters who have since turned to God and the faith of their parents have told me, "Their acceptance kept the channels open and made me want to hold on to my family."

But acts and attitudes of acceptance can do more than bridge and prevent potential rifts. Acceptance has a constructive power of its own. Carl Rogers emphasizes this in his book *On Becoming a Person* when he says, "If I accept the other person as something fixed, already diagnosed and classified, already shaped by his past, then I am doing my part to confirm this limited hypothesis. If I accept him as a process of becoming, then I am doing what I can to confer or make real his potentialities."

Applied to the hurting Christian parent situation, this means our rejection of our children could very well be solidifying their "unacceptable" positions. But by seeing and accepting them for what they could be—what God wants them to be—we may help confirm in them what they will be. Simply put, acceptance can prod our children to be more "acceptable."

This acceptance strategy is certainly biblical; the Lord recognizes and uses this power of acceptance to change lives. As Romans 5:8 reminds us, while we were still sinners, our hurting heavenly Father not only was willing to accept us, but he sent his Son to die to prove it. His spirit of acceptance provided the only way we could become acceptable. And his example is a powerful, challenging model for us as hurting parents.

A few years after *The Hurting Parent* was first published, two family counselors, Gary Smalley and John Trent, wrote an extremely helpful and insightful book entitled *The Blessing*. They fully develop the importance of parental acceptance in every person's life and relate it beautifully to the biblical model of a family "blessing." Application of their "blessing" model of acceptance could transform many hurting-parent/child relationships.

But acceptance is not the natural human reaction to hurt. Rejection would be far more natural; so would anger. We so often want acceptance to be conditional—based on the other person's response. As one mother told me, "Sometimes acceptance seems so unfair. I look at my son, and I can't help thinking, *He has rejected me and my standards and beliefs, so why should I have to accept him?*"

True acceptance has to start with a conscious decision on our part. And on occasion, as Bonnie Ahrens discovered, we may have to perform acts of acceptance before our feelings follow along. But God will honor those expressions. And I have learned from my own experiences that if we ask God for help, he will share some of his unlimited acceptance through us; we can in effect become agents of his acceptance.

I have also learned we can't take the strategy of acceptance for granted if we are genuinely concerned about maintaining or improving our relationships with our children. Acceptance forms the underpinnings, the essential starting point of any rebuilding, redemption, and reconciliation — for our heavenly Father and for every other parent.

SOMETHING TO THINK ABOUT

1. Why is acceptance so difficult? What hindrances to acceptance are illustrated in this chapter? What other hindrances could you add? What examples could you add?

2. When have you struggled with acceptance?

3. How would you explain the difference between acceptance and approval?

4. Think of an example of one of the benefits of acceptance you have experienced or heard about.

5. If you were going to build a biblical case for the importance and value of acceptance, what verses or Bible stories would you cite?

6. How does God show acceptance?

CHAPTER 6

ANGER

If anger is not restrained, it is frequently more hurtful
to us than the injury that provokes it.
—Seneca

Alice Skinner lay in the dark, listening for the crunch of tires on the gravel driveway. But the only sound she could hear was her husband's deep rhythmic breathing; Arnie was sound asleep.

How can he sleep as if nothing's wrong, she wondered, rolling over to check the digital clock on the nightstand. One o'clock—an hour later than their nineteen-year-old son, Kelly, promised he would be home.

A few moments later, Alice gently lifted the covers and got up. Pulling on the housecoat she had left draped over a chair, she slipped quietly out of the bedroom and into the hall. She walked carefully through the shadows and into the den, where she felt her way into her old wooden rocker. And there she sat in the darkness.

She had hoped this night would be different. But Kelly was late again. Alice and Arnie had made Kelly promise not to drink and drive or they wouldn't let him take the car. But she was sure he had broken that promise too. And she was scared. She couldn't get her mind off the eight kids who had been killed in alcohol-related accidents in the past year in the Skinners' small town.

She began to pray. "Lord, protect Kelly and bring him home safely."

After a few minutes, Alice flicked on the reading lamp beside the chair, retrieved the Bible off a nearby bookshelf, and started to read in the Psalms. But David's words did little to settle her mind.

Finally, there was a flash of headlights across the ceiling and she heard the engine shut off and the car door close. She laid the Bible on the reading table and waited for the den door to open.

Her son hadn't even stepped through the doorway when Alice bolted to her feet and demanded, "Where have you been? It's two o'clock in the morning."

Kelly mumbled something about a party at Allen's house and not realizing how late it was.

As Alice stepped toward him, she caught a whiff that confirmed her suspicions. All the long sleepless hours of worry came roaring to the surface in her loud accusation. "You've been drinking again!"

"I have not."

"Don't lie to me," she said. "You reek of beer. I can smell it. You've been drinking!" By now she was screaming at her son.

"I have not," Kelly retorted.

This second denial sent Alice into a rage. She charged at Kelly like a wild woman, flailing with her fists and screaming through her angry tears, "Don't you lie to me."

After absorbing the pounding of her first attack, Kelly retreated with his own fists clenched. Just then Arnie burst into the room.

He delivered a stern lecture to his son and ordered him to bed. To Alice, Arnie's words hardly seemed harsh enough. But then he hadn't been lying awake worrying, building up his fears and frustrations for the past three hours. In fact, he seemed surprised and bewildered by her violent reaction.

Alice, too, was shocked at her own outburst. How could she be reading her Bible and praying for her son one minute and attacking him the next? She tossed and turned most of the night, praying through silent tears, asking God to forgive her anger toward Kelly.

Yet despite her regrets, angry, early-morning homecomings became a pattern over the next few weeks. Whenever Kelly stayed out late, Alice began to worry. The inability to change his behavior gave her a helpless feeling that agitated those fears seething inside. By the time he got home, smelling of alcohol, Alice would be primed to explode.

"Eventually it sank in that my angry tantrums weren't doing any good at all," she said. "In fact, they were wreaking havoc with our family relationships. All my contacts with Kelly became strained. The atmosphere at home took on a hostile air. Sometimes when I'd get angry with Kelly, Arnie would defend him and the two of us would argue. Hostile feelings infected the entire family."

It shouldn't be surprising that so many hurting Christian parents struggle with angry reactions when dealing with children. Psychologists tell us anger is the instinctive human response to *fear*, *pain*, or *frustration*. Most of us parents have experienced a measure of all three.

Alice Skinner provided a good example of anger-prompting fear. So did the father who told me the following story: "I came home from work one day to find my twenty-year-old daughter, Patty, loading up a borrowed car with suitcases and small pieces of furniture from her room. Instantly, I realized what was happening and began to boil inside. I jumped out of my car, grabbed her around the waist, and dragged her, kicking and clawing, back into the house. Once inside, I let go. But she flew at me with pounding fists. So I grabbed her again, picked up her squirming 110 pounds, and dropped her roughly on the couch. And as she lay there screaming and crying in rage, I shouted out my own angry accusations and told her there was no way she was going to move in with her boyfriend as long as I lived.

"When I'd finally spent all my energy, and thought I'd won the battle, I left the room, leaving Patty silent but calm again on the couch.

"An hour later, I was changing clothes when I heard my wife, Norrine, come in the front door. Just then the phone rang. It was Patty. She had slipped away and was calling to tell her mother how I had bodily abused her by forcing her into the house and picking her up and throwing her on the couch. She said she'd been to the police station to sign a warrant against me.

" 'What's this all about?' my wife demanded when she had hung up. I told her I had caught Patty leaving the house, and as we had feared for some time, our daughter wanted to move in with her boyfriend. Norrine exploded and ran screaming through the house. I couldn't tell if she was angrier about Patty moving out or about the warrant.

"I was furious about both—so furious I couldn't feel anything but overpowering anger. But underlying it all was a terrible fear. I saw so many dangers. I was scared to death Patty was going to be hurt."

Life today, with its collapsing moral standards and changing norms, presents countless physical, emotional, and mental risks. Any parent has reason to fear for his or her children's protection. Christian parents experience the added fear of losing a son or daughter for eternity.

Fears often stem from our own experiences. We were young once; we went through independence struggles of our own. We made our mistakes, and in the years since we have seen many others make different mistakes. With insight and wisdom gained from age, observation, and painful personal history, we recognize more pitfalls than our children do. So whenever a son or daughter wanders a little too close to a danger area, we are understandably scared.

But many other fears arise out of our lack of experience, our inexperience with the world our children live in. We see media stories about drugs on high school campuses. Coed dorms have become an established fact at hundreds of colleges and universities. "Dorm brothels" is a descriptive term commonly used by some concerned counselors and educators. Our rapidly changing world offers many opportunities and temptations we never knew when we were young, and we feel absolutely helpless to deal with these issues we know nothing about. Because we can only imagine many of the now-generation dangers, these unknowns can create even greater fears than those pitfalls we have experienced and do understand.

All these dangers weigh heavily on a parent. And eventually, uncalmed fears find a way to express themselves. Often the way is anger.

Anger that results from hurt is perhaps the easiest to understand. Every hurting parent knows pain; and that feeling of personal pain can often cause an angry reaction. But sometimes Christian parents who maintain control of their own reactions to personal hurt react very angrily when a son or daughter hurts someone else — especially when the victim of the hurt is the other parent. This kind of anger prompted by concern for a husband or wife is easily justified. It is not really selfish, so it seems more permissible. But no matter the cause, anger is anger. The same dangers hold true. And we will discuss those dangers later in this chapter.

Frustration, the third prompter of anger, is another feeling hurting parents know a lot about. One of the most common frustrations was felt by the mother who related the following incident. "My oldest teenage daughter, coming home from school one day, stormed in the door and greeted me with the news, 'I don't believe the Bible anymore! I don't even believe in God!' Home alone in the quiet and peaceful atmosphere before the evening household rush, I was totally unprepared for her surprise attack. The shock set the adrenaline pumping, and I launched into an angry, loud, tongue-lashing defense of the Scripture and God Almighty. By the time I finished, there was nothing left for the Lord to say. I'd covered it all. In the aftermath of my angry outburst, all I could feel was frustration at the thought of fifteen long years of careful Christian training wasted."

Besides this common feeling that all our teaching has made no impact, hurting Christian parents experience other disappointments. For example, there are the frustrations of having children discount our views in favor of their peers' ideas, of having our children ignore our warnings of danger, of watching time wasted and life risked — and feeling helpless to do anything about any of it. The job of parenthood is frustrating enough at best, but add these problems and it is little wonder hurting Christian parents sometimes erupt in anger.

The symptoms of anger differ from parent to parent, of course. But open, expressed anger is the first type that comes to mind. Alice Skinner exemplified this when she screamed at her son the moment he set foot in the house after a night on the town. Such verbally biting anger is not an uncommon experience for hurting Christian parents. Many of them confess to living in a stormy atmosphere of continuous hostility where the verbal Armageddons are merely the flare-ups in a running battle routinely marked by bickering and sniping.

Physical fighting is probably the exception rather than the rule. But it does occur. I have heard stories that varied from the mother who broke a broom over the back of her son during an argument, to the minister who beat his seventeen-year-old son so severely the boy needed to be hospitalized.

But not all acted-out anger leads to violence and bloody brawls. Most hurting parents can express their anger in more creative ways.

"My son's smoking used to infuriate me so," one mother said. "When I'd see the shape of a cigarette pack in his shirt pocket, I'd clench my hand and mash it against his chest, twisting my fist until I could feel the cigarettes crumple."

Another parent admitted acting out his anger by deliberately inconveniencing his son. When the boy would come home after curfew, this father would lock the door and refuse to let him in. The son had a choice of sleeping in the car or waking up a friend and spending the night with him.

Much of the anger felt by hurting Christian parents, however, is not expressed at all. It is hidden, suppressed, because of guilt. Yet as a smoldering, muzzled emotion, this inner anger is no less real, as was shown in the experience of one wealthy Christian couple whose only son planned to marry without his parents' blessing. The mother argued heatedly with the boy every time the subject came up. Eventually, every conversation, whatever the subject, ended in a mother-son shouting match. The father stayed out of those fights. But when questioned concerning his feelings about his son's plans, he replied matter-of-factly, "The day he gets married I'm writing him out of my will." His anger, though more restrained than his wife's, was just as strong.

Sometimes the emotion smoldering inside has to find a subconscious outlet. One mother whose daughter was living with a boyfriend shared her example, saying, "One night at the supper table my husband forced me to face my inner hostilities. 'You know,' he observed, 'whenever we call Barb and Jeff answers the phone, we just ask to speak to Barb. We never so much as say hello to Jeff. Doesn't that strike you as rude?'

"My first response was, 'I never thought of it that way.' But later, as I pondered my husband's comment, I had to admit to myself that my shortness with Jeff on the phone had been a subconscious expression of my true feelings. For a long time I thought I had my anger under control because I didn't express it. But the spite was still there inside."

Anger is not a reaction that hurting parents can afford to ignore. We can't pass off the occasional tirade or vindictive punishment as merely a harmless outburst of temper any more than we can smother those inner hostilities by pretending we have our feelings under control.

The explosions of intrafamily warfare create dangerously unpredictable fallout. A sobering illustration of this was told me by the father whose sixteen-year-old daughter, Cori, ran away from home. She returned ten days later a sorry sight. She obviously hadn't had a shower or shampoo in days. An ugly red streak was visible through a hole torn in the leg of her jeans. Cori's mother insisted on inspecting the red streak on her leg, but Cori refused.

"That's when I blew up," her father said. "She struck at me, and I swung back — harder than I intended. One of my blows actually added a black eye to her other bruises."

Later, after taking Cori to the doctor for treatment of her blood poisoning, this father began to suffer terrible guilt for hitting his daughter. "Sure, she had some punishment coming," he said, "but my anger had burst out of control. So right away I asked Cori and God to forgive me."

Cori and her father began rebuilding their relationship after that. Several years and numerous ups and downs later, Cori is a Christian today. But that's not the whole story. The final repercussions weren't discovered until six years after Cori's runaway scene. Joni, a younger daughter, who was by then a teenager, disappeared one day when she left home on a household errand. Hours passed before her parents found her at the house of one of her friends several miles away. On the way back home, they talked to Joni about the cause of her unhappiness. Together they agreed to relieve the pressures Joni felt at home. Then Joni hesitantly confessed, "Something has bothered me for a long time. Remember that time Cori ran away when I was little and when she came home Daddy beat up on her and made her all black and blue and red all over?"

Her father gasped. *Oh God, has she thought for all those years that I did all that to Cori?*

"Joni, let's talk about that," he said. And immediately he called a family sharing time. He figured if the incident had bothered Joni, the other children probably had their own questions.

There, in the living room, this father explained what had happened with Cori and admitted his part of the blame. He told about the guilt he had felt and about asking for forgiveness.

"Thank God we finally got everything out in the open," he said. But in the meantime there is no way to tell how much damage had been caused in his relationships with his other children as a result of the fallout from that one angry scene.

Open expressions of anger have another danger—they cause callousness. Every shouting match, every disciplinary decision spurred by anger inflicts a wound. And every new wound heals over with a tougher scar tissue. Each time the combatants have to get a little angrier, probe a little deeper, scream a little louder, hit a little harder to make the same impact.

"I remember one time my father came into my room and found me reading a paperback book he didn't approve of," one young man told me.

"He went into a rage, grabbed the book out of my hands, and ripped it up. I didn't say anything. But this irrational anger seemed so fascist to me that I said to myself, 'Go ahead, Hitler! Tear up my books.' I increased the stubborn determination to read what I chose."

Vented anger always flames hostility, resentment, and bitterness. One of the best examples of this I ever heard concerned a woman who wrote a scathing letter to a son who had ignored her wishes by withdrawing from a Bible school and enrolling in a state university.

She blistered him all the way through the letter before bitterly concluding that she prayed each day God would cause him to have an automobile accident to place him at the brink of death in a hospital bed. Then he would have to reconsider his evil ways and repent for what he was putting his parents through.

In the margin of the letter, she angrily wrote a Bible reference: "The fear of the LORD is the beginning of knowledge: but fools despise wisdom and instruction. My son, hear the instruction of thy father, and forsake not the law of thy mother" (Prov. 1:7–8 KJV).

More than twenty years have passed since this mother's angry letter. But the hostilities expressed in her letter and in other flare-ups have created a massive chasm between this mother and her son. He hasn't been home since he received the letter. And her continued bitterness and anger merely fuel his cynicism toward God and Christianity.

Unexpressed anger can be just as harmful. It is a hidden malignancy that may grow into hatred if it isn't dealt with. I expect most readers will protest, "I couldn't hate one of my children." But you could if you harbored angry feelings for any length of time.

The malignancy of unexpressed anger not only can worsen into hatred, but can spread, affecting more and more of a parent's life. The anger felt toward a prodigal child is often turned inward to become anger at oneself. (We will deal with this idea in greater depth in chapter 8.)

Another problem was alluded to in the opening case of this chapter. Alice Skinner's feeling of anger began to crop up in her relationship with her husband. Marital tensions have a way of growing when any strain is imposed. But when the cause of the strain is something as important to us as a son or daughter, the tension can be multiplied.

Other parents have confessed to me that their anger or irritation with one rebellious child made them irritable with their other children who weren't causing any hurt. This kind of transference is especially dangerous for hurting parents because it can compound problems and even create problems in relationships that were previously problem-free.

How can a hurting Christian parent deal with the anger he or she feels toward a son or daughter who has rejected the parent's teachings and beliefs?

A psychologist friend, W. Curry Mavis, wrote in *The Holy Spirit in the Christian Life*: "Christians normally have a sense of shame when they become angry, and they have strong tendencies to deny and repress distraught feelings. The first step in handling angry feelings creatively is to acknowledge them. This step cannot be bypassed."

It is also good therapy to admit our anger to someone else, our spouse, another hurting Christian parent, or a counselor. The act of admitting emotion often helps us control it.

When we do misuse our anger, when we direct it at the personhood of our children instead of their behavior, the appropriate guilt we then feel should help keep us in line. It should prompt us to ask for forgiveness—from God and from our children.

But by far the best way to deal with any troublesome emotion is to replace it with something else. And that is the positive emphasis we will cover in the next chapter.

SOMETHING TO THINK ABOUT

1. What are the three prompters of anger highlighted in this chapter? Can you name any other triggers of anger? Which trigger seems most common in your experience?

2. Look back at the various illustrations in this chapter and try to decide which of the three triggers seemed most prevalent in each parent's case.

3. What (if anything) is the difference between anger at a person and anger at a behavior? How would you try to express that difference to avoid misunderstandings?

4. Is anger ever redemptive? Explain your answer.

CHAPTER 7

UNCONDITIONAL LOVE

Many waters cannot quench love; rivers cannot wash it away.
—Song of Songs 8:7

The Farrones preferred to stay near home on holidays to avoid heavy traffic. So they spent a beautiful Labor Day afternoon playing golf at their club and ended the day with a picnic supper for the family—the whole family except Tony.

As their celebration ended and Carol Farrone quietly cleared the paper plates off the picnic table, her mind turned to her son. That was the way it always was; she could push aside the thoughts for only a little while before the wonderings and worries began to haunt her again. Now another holiday had passed with no word.

Preparing for bed later that evening, Carol voiced her concern to her husband, Joe. "It would surely be great if Tony would call."

Joe patted his wife's arm. "It would be nice to at least know where he is."

Joe was taking a shower when the phone rang. Carol picked up the receiver to hear an operator say, "I have a collect call from Tony Farrone. Will you accept charges?"

Before Carol could finish saying she would be glad to accept the call, a weak voice on the other end of the line broke in. "Hi, Mom."

"It's wonderful to hear your voice, honey. Where are you?" Carol asked.

As Tony answered, his feeble words began to fade. "I'm so sick, Mom, and so hungry. I'm really hurting. Tell me what to do."

Carol strained to try to catch her son's last words. Then a strong, businesslike voice boomed into her ear, "Ma'am, your son came dragging into my lobby here a few minutes ago and begged me to let him use our phone to call you. He is in bad shape, and he is here at the Holiday Inn." The man named a city 150 miles from the Farrones' home.

"You don't know how much I appreciate your kindness, sir," Carol told the man on the phone. "May I ask one more favor? If you could just put him up in a room, I promise we'll be there first thing in the morning to pick him up and pay you for the room and all your trouble."

But before the man could respond, Joe Farrone picked up an extension phone and interrupted. "Sir, we'll leave immediately to come and get him. He needs us now. Please keep him there for us."

Within ten minutes the entire Farrone family piled into their car and took off. (When the two teenage girls learned Tony had called, they wanted to go too.) The three-hour drive was a long haul after a tiring day, but an overwhelming feeling of relief rejuvenated them.

They knew without being told that Tony was on drugs again. But at least they finally knew where he was. And that knowledge gave them glad release from the torturous anxiety. It was far easier to deal with the reality of the drugs than the chronic uncertainty and suspense of the preceding months.

The Farrones pulled to a stop as close as they could get to the entrance of the Holiday Inn. As they entered and approached the desk, they spotted Tony across the lobby, sprawled on a couch, obviously strung out. Carol and Joe rushed to their son's side. "We're here, dear," Carol whispered. "It's Mom and Dad. We're going to take you home."

It was minutes before Tony rose close enough to consciousness to realize who was talking. A corpse couldn't have looked more lifeless. His dirt-caked, matted hair hung across his sticky face. His ragged, sweat-soaked clothes were covered with filth from long days on the road. He had worn holes in the soles of both shoes.

Joe went to the desk to settle with the night manager and thank him for the call. The man's pity was penetrating. Joe could read the expression on his face as clearly as if the man had said, "You poor people. You're so different from what I expected. You're not scum at all."

After his numerous fruitless attempts to pull himself up, the Farrones realized Tony couldn't make it to the car by himself. So Carol, Joe, and the two girls gently and lovingly shared his weight as they carried him out of the lobby and across the parking lot in the stillness of the early morning hours.

After his father had strapped him into the front seat, Tony slumped to his side and sank into unconsciousness. His father placed a loving arm on Tony's shoulder and tenderly said, "You're having a rough time of it, aren't you, Son?"

Tony stirred but made no response.

Joe hadn't driven a block before the stench of their son got to the Farrones. The perspiration of days and maybe weeks of hitchhiking combined with the vomit of recent hours was more than they could bear. They had to cover their noses and open the car windows for ventilation.

"I remember thinking as I drove home," Joe said, "I've heard so many sermons about the prodigal son in a stinking pigpen. Now here I am holding my nose and living out that very scene. But what really hit me was how thankful the prodigal's father must have felt.

"And then the thought: *My son. I love him because he is my son. He has come back home, and that's all that matters now.*"

Once home, the loving thankfulness turned to loving care. The family physician warned that Tony's dehydration had to be corrected immediately; getting liquids into his body was crucial.

So for three days Carol and Joe Farrone gently force-fed their son as if he were a helpless baby. They held open his mouth and dropped in juices. Finally, Tony regained enough strength to care for his own basic personal needs. But it took a month of tender loving care to bring him back to the place where he could function once more on his own.

This Farrones' experience vividly illustrates what I feel is the most powerful resource hurting Christian parents can use. That resource is unconditional love.

Parental love can be powerful; it is instinctive up to a point. But unconditional love is even more powerful; and it is not instinctive. In fact, it is downright unnatural. Unconditional love is the kind of love the Farrones showed that Labor Day evening when they got the call for help from their strung-out son. Theirs was a love without reservation or prerequisites. It demanded no reciprocation, no reward — not even a response.

I think of one couple, a pastor and his wife, whom I met at a speaking engagement in Alabama. Their son had been out riding one night when the guys he was with decided to hold up a store. The group was caught, the minister's son was implicated because he was with the others, and all the boys were sent to prison. Every week of the year, this couple drives the one hundred miles from their home to visit their son in prison. The boy, who knows how embarrassed his parents are about his crime, is so ashamed of himself that he regularly tells his parents they don't need to come so often. But the next week they go back. And on holidays, such as Thanksgiving and Christmas, they drive to the prison and eat their special holiday meal with their son in the prison cafeteria. They do it, they tell their son, because they love him. The boy can't doubt it, because their actions underline their words.

In researching this book, and in the years since it first came out, I have come across numerous miracles worked through the unconditional love of hurting parents. And in every case the parents shared at least one thing in common with the Farrones and this Alabama couple—an active love. Their affection was more than an attitude. It was acted out. Active love travels long distances in the middle of the night to rescue a deathly sick son or to visit a child in prison; it writes letter after letter without waiting for a response; it enthusiastically hugs a son who only reluctantly accepts affection.

Like the acceptance we discussed earlier, love, to be effective, needs to be unmistakably obvious. It is not enough to offer the lame argument, "Of course they know we love them. They're our kids."

Verbalizing love gives it impact. But words aren't enough either. If Joe and Carol Farrone had just told their son they loved him and hung up, he very possibly wouldn't be alive today. And if we as hurting parents don't continue to express our love to our children in words and actions, there is no way to know where they will be tomorrow.

One of the most overlooked means of expressing love to young adult children is physical affection. Most of us hand out plenty of this when our kids are young. But as they grow up, we hesitate to express much if any of the intimacy we provided when they were small. And as differences and hurts separate us, it gets easier and easier to curtail all physical contact. Yet psychologists tell us every human being craves and needs physical affection. A kiss, a hug, a gentle squeeze, a soft touch on the arm can speak powerfully and eloquently of love.

Unfortunately, many hurting Christian parents never get down to acting out their love because they are hung up with guilt over the fact they don't always feel the love they know should be there. They go through the anguish one respected Christian author and teacher did when his unmarried daughter came home one day and said she was pregnant.

"The resentment against her was so strong that my deepest feelings were closer to hatred than to love," this father confessed. "Yet I felt so wrong. I'd always preached love and had even written a book about John Wesley's concept of perfect love."

What this man came to know and what every hurting Christian parent needs to remember is that unconditional love is not always an overwhelming, uncontrollable feeling. It is more than just an emotion or a heartfelt warmth. Unconditional love is a conscious choice. And sometimes, when the feelings sag, it may be mostly resolve. It is as much a matter of the mind and will as of the heart.

Further evidence of this is the apostle Paul's description of love in 1 Corinthians 13. He didn't discuss the subject in ethereal, emotional, or philosophical terms. He defined love with a practical list of what it did or didn't do.

Henry Drummond, in *The Greatest Thing in the World*, his classic commentary on the Bible's love chapter, breaks love down into a number of ingredients. Many of these speak directly to hurting Christian parents.

Patience. Sometimes not acting is an act of love. In fact, Drummond says patience "is the normal attitude of love; love passive, love waiting to begin; not in a hurry; calm; ready to do its work when the summons comes." That certainly describes the Farrones, as well as many other hurting parents who have already shared in the pages of this book.

One mother who typifies patient love said, "We've been waiting years for a time when our son Adam needed us. But any attention or love from us has always been rebuffed. He accused us of favoritism and even refused to attend his brother's wedding. Adam wouldn't cooperate when we wanted a complete family portrait. He would refuse to get together with the rest of the family when we wanted to celebrate a holiday together. But we never quit trying to include him and show our love.

"Now after eight years of marriage his wife has divorced him. In his sorrow, he has come home to live with us. This is the chance we've been waiting for to prove our love. He needs us now."

Kindness. If patience is love waiting, kindness is love active. It is often so simple, but it is the most obvious and effective expression of love. Think about Jesus. How much of his ministry was spent doing things for the people he met? He set an example for us and then challenged us with the assurance that any kindness done "to the least of these" was the highest brand of service we could offer him.

One mother I know, in an attempt to show her continued love for her unmarried son, sometimes takes a plate of freshly baked cookies by the apartment where he and his girlfriend live.

A seminary student told me, "When I was eighteen and went into partnership with a buddy to buy a tavern, it nearly broke Dad's heart. But he and Mom always expected me to come home for special Sunday dinner. And he was always ready to drive across town and help me fix my car when it wouldn't start. This demonstrated love was what kept me open to them and to God and helped bring me back to where I am today."

Kind acts take real effort and determination in the face of our hurts and concerns, but they are essential. Our expressions and claims of love ring hollow without kindness.

Humility. There is a great temptation for parents to use love to appeal to their children in order to manipulate them into conformity or guilt. The martyrdom routine does this: "Look how much I'm willing to do for you in spite of the way you've treated me."

But love that flaunts itself like that is not unconditional, because it demands attention and gratitude. The love Paul writes about "vaunteth not itself" (v. 4 KJV). Its hiddenness by no means limits its power. If any love is limited, it is the limelight love, because its demands for notice can create resentments or barriers. Humble love is free to work gently, unoffensively, behind the scenes, unencumbered by the need to be noticed.

Courtesy. "Love doth not behave itself unseemly" (v. 5 KJV) is the way Paul put it. Drummond elaborated on the point when he defined politeness as "love in trifles."

But if there is one place where a Christian's common courtesy breaks down, it is in the home. Parents often interrupt a son or daughter to get their own opinions stated. We often don't devote full attention when our children talk or extend them the courtesy of hearing them out. We are just as likely to demand and expect instant obedience as we are to tack on a polite "please" or "thank you." We even correct and sometimes criticize our children in front of guests in our home. In summary, we can too easily shed our manners like wet boots when we cross the threshold of our own homes.

I can't help wondering what would happen if every hurting Christian parent suddenly began treating his or her children with the same courtesy and respect given to a non-Christian neighbor or friend at work. That would show love.

Unselfishness. We often think of unselfishness as meaning the giving up of our rights. Drummond says, "Love strikes much deeper. It would have us not seek them at all, ignore them, eliminate the personal element altogether." Unselfish, unconditional love is love without calculation.

A hurting parent can look at a son or a daughter and justifiably argue, "What about the commandment to honor parents? Doesn't my child owe me some respect?" Yes, but that is the child's responsibility. If our love is truly unconditional, we will ignore and even forget those rights. We will just love unselfishly without thought about what is due us.

A most impressive example of this kind of sacrificial love is a minister and his wife who were serving a small rural church in the Deep South a few years ago. They had a bright, attractive daughter who was a joy to their lives until she entered high school and began dating mostly older, more experienced boys. The more concerned her parents became about her relationships, the more rebellious and wild she became.

These parents had held high hopes for their daughter, but little by little they watched her abandon their educational dreams and goals in an attempt to melt into the provincial atmosphere of her little rural school. When she fell in love with a senior boy of questionable character and negligible ambition, her parents decided to act.

The father resigned his church and moved his family to a New England community with a highly respected school district, where his daughter could get a first-rate education and exposure to a more enriching environment. He moved despite the fact he knew he wouldn't find a church to serve. He was primarily a self-taught man, and the churches in their new community required men with seminary training. So he gave up regular ministry and took other work to support his family and to provide his daughter with the kind of environment he thought best for her.

"If we hadn't moved," said the daughter, "I'd be pumping gas and helping my husband manage some little corner station in a little Mississippi crossroads town, far from where God wants me to be."

Instead, she is a respected Christian author and speaker with a beautiful Christian family and an immense debt of gratitude to a hurting father who willingly surrendered his own career out of concern and love for her.

Good temper. Paul's Corinthian letter says love "is not easily provoked" (v. 5 KJV). When he adds, "Love does not keep a record of wrongs," he touches on a strategy that is a great aid to good temper and is elaborated on in chapter 9 on forgiveness.

But as stated in chapter 6 on anger, there is no effective way to change ill temper; it has to be replaced. As Drummond puts it, "Souls are made sweet not by taking the acid fluids out but by putting something in—a great love, a new spirit, the Spirit of Christ." The feelings of ill temper that plague hurting Christian parents have to be flushed out and kept out by an overflowing spirit of good-tempered love.

The final two ingredients Drummond lists for love are *gentleness* and *sincerity*, which are his expressions for Paul's phrases, "thinketh no evil" and "rejoiceth in the truth."

Love that thinks no evil, in Drummond's words, "imputes no motives, sees the bright side, puts the best construction on every action. What a delightful state of mind to live in!"

One mother whose son moved away from home after months of conflict over his lifestyle didn't hear from the boy for some time after he moved into his own apartment. "Every day I thought about calling him to find out how he was to show my love by expressing an interest," she said. "But I kept waiting to see if he would call home. Each day I would get more discouraged and feel more certain he was trying to make us worry. So each day I became angrier and more determined to wait and see how long he would go without calling.

"After three weeks I could stand the anger and the worry no longer. I called, and when my son answered the phone, I could hardly believe his warmth. It was the best conversation we had had in months. He even apologized for not calling sooner. When we concluded and I hung up, I felt ashamed. I'd gotten myself all riled up by reading malice into my son's behavior. It was such a relief to learn the truth."

"Love thinketh no evil."

But this is tough, if not almost impossible for a discouraged Christian parent to do. In our humanness we tend to blame our children for intentionally cruel motives. And we are apt to be pessimists who see the worst possible consequences for everything.

A father of a rebellious daughter proved the exception to the pessimism rule when the girl called late one night with the news she had been kicked out of her Christian college for breaking the rules. There was a long silence on that long-distance line.

Then the father said, "Well, Cindy, I guess you'd better catch the next plane home." He paused then gently continued, "And remember, when you stand back a distance from a picture, it is usually the dark lines that give it character and beauty."

This father didn't accuse his daughter of foolishness or berate her for her inconsiderate waste of a quarter's worth of time or tuition money. He didn't say, "I told you so," even though he had seen the trouble coming. His unconditional love enabled him to see the bright side and, in so doing, express his continued love and faith in his daughter despite her troubles.

Cindy's father understood what Drummond meant when he said, "If we try to influence or elevate others, we shall soon see that success is in proportion to their belief in our belief in them. The respect of another is the first restoration of the self-respect a man has lost; our ideal of what he is becomes to him the hope and pattern of what he may become."

Unconditional love that sees the positive pays off. Because of her father's confidence and trust in her, Cindy went back to school the next quarter. She buckled down to her studies, eventually committed her life to God, and served a term as a missionary in South America. She wrote me some time ago to say she was working as a family counselor in a mental health agency and regularly lending out her personal copy of *The Hurting Parent* to clients she thought could benefit from it.

The kind of love that embodies all the ingredients we have mentioned—patience, kindness, humility, courtesy, unselfishness, good temper, gentleness, and sincerity—doesn't just happen when and if we decide we are going to be more loving. It is more a goal to aim for than it is a strategy we can easily adopt. Even with hard work and practice, it is humanly impossible.

One mother voiced her frustration at the inadequacy of human love when she told me, "We have loved. We have cared until our health is broken. We have been taken advantage of. We have been robbed of possessions and money. The drug addiction gets worse than anything we ever dreamed or imagined. We're to the point now we have to guard our billfolds in our own home. Sometimes the human love flees and leaves us with empty hurt. Then all we can do is cry, 'Oh God! Give us love.'"

Here's where I probably need to clarify what this chapter is saying. Unconditional love doesn't mean "anything goes" or "we'll just have to grin and bear it." There are times when establishing firm and healthy behavioral boundaries is essential to protecting ourselves and also for confronting a wrongdoer with his or her need to change. Not doing so may result in enablement or codependency.

As acknowledged in chapter 4 on rejection, there is sometimes the need for "tough love" or perhaps even direct psychological, medical, or legal intervention. But setting firm limits on behavior doesn't have to mean setting limits on our love. As difficult as it might be (1) to declare that no further money or aid will be provided; (2) to remove a grandchild from the custody of a wayward son or daughter who is abusive, unfaithful, neglected, or addicted; or even (3) to turn a prodigal son or daughter over to the police, it is possible to do any of those things or to take many another firm stand—not in anger, guilt, shame, or frustration, but in the spirit of unconditional love.

Sound impossible? Remember we're not talking about ordinary human love. Fortunately, the Lord's brand of unconditional love is a better quality than any we could produce on our own. In 1 Corinthians 13:7 Paul claims this "love never gives up: and its faith, hope, and patience never fail" (TEV). That's the kind of love we need to tap into.

And one of the best illustrations I have heard on this persistent side of love involved some friends of mine, Ben and Ella Johnson. For several years after their son Jack married Sue, Ben and Ella had a warm, normal relationship with their daughter-in-law, until one day, for some inexplicable reason, Sue turned cold. She began avoiding her in-laws and refusing to communicate with them. And soon Jack, too, shut his parents out of his life.

Time after time Ben and Ella asked what was wrong, what they had done to hurt Jack and Sue, what they could do to make it up. But there was never an explanation.

One of the hardest things for Ben and Ella to bear was the reaction of Jack and Sue's children—their own grandsons. When Ben would see the boys on the streets of their small town, they would deliberately look the other way. Ella would bump into one of her grandsons in a store, and he would walk away when she tried to speak to him.

For years the Christmas and birthday gifts the Johnsons sent Jack's family would be returned unopened. They tried sending cards with checks enclosed, only to have no acknowledgment and the checks not cashed.

"It was such a tightly closed door," Ben said. "But we couldn't give up."

They tried all kinds of loving gestures. Ella took them fresh bread or rolls, strawberry jam, and other things a mother enjoys sharing. But each offer was met with refusal.

"Ben and I would talk and talk, trying to imagine what we'd done," Ella said. "We were always hoping and praying our love would someday find a way to breach the empty chasm between us and our son's family. I would say, 'Ben, do you think if I would do this or ask that or take Jack and Sue some other thing, it would help?'

"Things finally came to the point where Ben responded, 'Do you just want to keep getting hurt? Don't we hurt enough?'

"But we knew we had to risk it. Neither of us wanted to give up."

After a financial crisis, Jack and Sue sold their farm with plans to move hundreds of miles away. The day the moving van came, Ella went to their house once more, in a final expression of love. This time she took a box of candy for Jack's family to eat on their trip and Jack's prized old high school yearbooks he had left at home when he got married.

Ella's spirits soared with new hope when Jack accepted the candy and the yearbooks and even thanked his mother. Her determined love was heartened. But when she and Ben continued to send cards and gifts for birthdays and special occasions, those expressions of love were still returned.

Three years later the Johnsons planned a long trip that was to take them through the state where Jack and Sue lived. "We couldn't think of going so near without telling them about our plans," Ella said. So she wrote a letter.

A few days later she got a reply. Sue wrote to ask them to please stop for a visit on their trip.

"What a day!" Ella said. "We cried and thanked God."

Naturally, Ben and Ella spent the first two weeks of their trip in excited anticipation of the time they would arrive at Jack and Sue's new home. Before they left their motel room on the morning of the appointed day, the Johnsons held a special time of prayer. Ben wept as he asked God to help them show their love to Jack and Sue and the grandchildren and to give them a beautiful time of reunion.

"As we drove that day, we admitted to each other our uneasiness," Ella remembered. "We wondered if Sue might wish she hadn't invited us. But we had prayed so long for that day, and we knew friends were praying too. So we were confident God was preparing the way."

The minute Ben and Ella pulled into their son's driveway, their car was surrounded by the smiling faces of Jack, Sue, and the grandchildren. The entire family ushered Ben and Ella on a tour of the house and made them feel warmly welcome. The ten years of unexplained alienation had finally ended.

Today, though the long years of hurt still remain a mystery to them, Ben and Ella have rebuilt a loving relationship with their son and his family. But neither of these long-suffering parents believes the breach ever could have been bridged without the persistent love they refused to give up.

In their struggle with despair, Ben and Ella found no human resources that could supply the kind of unconditional love they needed to get through to their son and daughter-in-law. But they found, as any hurting Christian parent who asks can find, that God has an abundant supply of love. And he is willing to supply all we can use.

Paul wrote about this love source when he said:

> I pray that Christ will be more and more at home in your hearts, living within you as you trust in him. May your roots go down deep into the soil of God's marvelous love; and may you be able to feel and understand, as all God's children should, how long, how wide, how deep and how high his love really is; and to experience this love for yourselves, though it is so great that you will never see the end of it or fully know or understand it. And so at last you will be filled up with God himself. (Eph. 3:17 – 19 TLB)

That is the only secret to the kind of unconditional love that can have an impact on the lives of our children.

SOMETHING TO THINK ABOUT

1. What examples of unconditional parental love can you find in the Bible?

2. List the adjectives used in this chapter to define unconditional parental love. Add examples of your own. Add other helpful adjectives that could be used.

3. When do you find it hardest to feel and exhibit this kind of unconditional love? With which one of Drummond's characteristics of unconditional love do you have the most difficulty?

4. What examples of unconditional love have you seen or heard about in hurting parents?

5. How do you act loving when you don't feel especially loving?

CHAPTER 8

GUILT

From the body of one guilty deed
a thousand ghostly fears and haunting thoughts proceed.
—Wordsworth

Dick Manville trusted his daughter Marie. At age nineteen she was still very much a daddy's girl. And unlike her older brothers, she had never given her folks a moment's trouble. Dick never worried about her relationship with her boyfriend, Andy, either—until the morning Dick came down to the kitchen for an early breakfast and saw Marie at the sink. She slipped something into her mouth and washed it down with a swallow of orange juice. She started when she heard his footsteps on the linoleum floor. He offered a cheery "good morning" on his way to the table and started to ask if Marie had a headache this early in the day. But as he passed her open purse on the counter, he saw them—next to her compact was a dispenser of birth control pills.

The headache question lodged in his throat. And he could only manage a halfhearted "Have a good day, honey" a moment later when Marie announced she was off for work. He was still motionless at the table, wondering if he had really seen what he had seen, when his wife, Martha, came in ten minutes later to fix breakfast. He didn't tell her why he wasn't hungry.

Dick went to the office. But all he could think about were those pills and their implications. *That means Andy and Marie ... How long?* Not a paper moved on Dick's desk all morning.

By noon guilt had set in. Dick felt a sickening responsibility for Marie's sexual involvement. He berated himself for being so lax in the restrictions he had placed on her. Why hadn't he said something when Marie had started turning down dates with other guys to date Andy?

As he reviewed the past few years, a number of parental mistakes flashed like bright neon signs in his mind. And he sank further into guilt with the thought that he should have realized them all before.

After a week of plaguing guilt, Dick talked himself into broaching the subject with Marie. After all, he was her father; he was responsible. The least he could do was discuss with Marie her relationship with Andy. But the attempt failed miserably. He and Marie talked, but Dick could never quite bring the real issue into focus. And when their discussion ended, Dick felt guiltier than ever for failing again.

The more Dick thought about his guilt in this matter with Marie, the more he wondered about his older kids. They all professed to be Christians, but none of them was really moving or growing in the Lord. He began to feel that somewhere, somehow he had failed as a Christian father.

He finally told Martha what he knew about their daughter. And he confessed his own guilt and self-doubts. Martha tried to encourage him, arguing that he had been a wonderful father and saying she knew all the kids felt that way. But Dick refused to listen to her assurances.

The guilt was worst when he would lie awake in bed at night waiting for Marie to come home from a date. He wondered where she was and what she was doing. And he would examine his life in search of every mistake he had made as a father.

I should have spent more time with Marie. Maybe if I hadn't traveled so much and left Martha to raise the kids. We should have insisted she date only boys from the church. Did we let her start dating too soon? If only we'd talked about dating and relationships more openly.... I've been negligent in so many areas.

Dick Manville's guilt mounted as the weeks passed. It loomed over him like a mountain of depression, crippling every relationship in his life—with Marie, with his wife, Martha, with his colleagues at work, and even with God. He withdrew into his own private world of suffering.

"The guilt gripped me like some sort of demonic force," he said. "I felt overwhelmed by oppression I couldn't shake. And I began to take on the troubled and tormented personality of an oppressed, guilty person."

Each hurting Christian parent wrestles with his or her own measure of guilt. But there are no more perfect parents than there are perfect people. We have all committed parental sins for which we are rightfully to blame.

Our guilt often churns up memories of inconsistencies in our own spiritual lives. The more we remember, the more we wonder if our own shortcomings could be to blame for the problems of our children.

One mother who anguishes over her daughter's lack of interest in church said, "I feel guilty because I remember how seldom we could get our family assembled to read the Bible and pray together. We used to insist she go to Sunday school, but my husband and I often stayed home and took our time getting ready for the eleven o'clock worship service. I can't help wondering if our lackadaisical attitude is the reason she gave up on God."

Guilt works like a DVR with an infinite memory that refuses to forget the mistakes we have made as parents. It plays them over and over again in our minds, in slow motion and from every conceivable angle.

One father told me he feels guilty now because he is convinced he used the wrong disciplinary tactics on one of his sons. "Looking back I can see he was different from our other kids. He needed more love and assurance than the others. But I tried to dole out those things in equal measure," he said. "He was a sensitive boy who would have responded better to love. But I badgered and hounded him and tried to force him into the same mold as our other kids. I realize now the damage I did to our relationship and to him as a person. I feel guilty because I know I caused much of his rebellion."

Bruce and Millie Crane, whose story is told in chapter 5 on acceptance, also struggled with guilt because of mistakes they made when Andrea was a young girl. The early years of their family life had been stormy, their marriage shaky. Andrea had suffered from some of the effects of her parents' early troubles. When a little sister had been born with a physical defect, Bruce and Millie had left Andrea in the care of another family for several weeks while they were gone for their baby's surgery. It wasn't until they returned home that they realized what terrible emotional damage had been done to Andrea by their leaving her and by the treatment of the family she stayed with.

"In the years of her young adult rebellion," Bruce Crane said, "we couldn't escape the feelings of guilt as we wondered how many of Andrea's problems stemmed back to that time in her childhood."

All of us look back over our years of parenthood and find real, justified reasons for our guilt. But I have discovered that much, if not most, of the guilt that plagues hurting mothers and fathers is unnecessary, false guilt.

For years, from the moment a son or daughter is born, our sense of parental responsibility demands we control or answer for that child's actions. It is just a habitual part of our duty as parents; we almost instinctively view our children as extensions of our own persons. This is why most of us have a difficult time relinquishing our feeling of responsibility for a child's decisions and behavior. But there comes a time when we have to let this go. As we allow a child a growing independence, we also have to wean ourselves from accountability.

I have talked to some parents who refuse to do this. Their young adult children are independent in every other way, but the mother and father still blame themselves for any sins the children commit. We need to realize some things are beyond our control. In many cases, it's not that the parenting was lacking or weak, but the world's temptations and attractions are so strong. The failure to realize this produces unnecessary guilt.

An overabundance of introspection can also create enormous false guilt. Dick Manville was certainly a graphic example of this. The more closely he examined his life as a father, the more guilt he felt. He amplified the impact of his mistakes beyond all reason. As Dick spent more and more time drawing causal lines between the past and the present, he began to entertain thoughts of what might have been. And soon, like so many other hurting parents, he was suffering from a chronic case of the "if onlies."

Of course it is a natural reaction for a hurting parent to reexamine himself or herself in search of some explanation. But too much and too close a scrutiny, with the magnification of hindsight, can blow many things out of proportion. We begin to dwell on what went wrong and overlook what went right. The result is an overload of unwarranted guilt.

Relatives, friends, and other observers often heap on extra false guilt when they offer simplistic suggestions, make uninformed judgments, or in some other way unintentionally imply parental blame. They never know what damage they do to the parents' spirits.

One father recalled for me an incident where he shared his hurt about an estranged son with his own parents. "My folks didn't have any idea of how to help me or my son," he said. "But Dad thought for a while, then commented, 'You must have done something to bring this on.' Dad will never know how that hurt me. I needed his encouragement and support, not his judgment. I already had so much guilt of my own that his comment was almost more than I could take right then."

Another source of false guilt is something we already touched on in the chapter on isolation — the pressures of the American success syndrome. We read how-to books on raising a Christian family and wonder where we went wrong. We sit through Mother's Day and Father's Day sermons glorifying the greatness of parenthood. Then we compare ourselves and our families with those around us, and we feel guilty if we don't seem to measure up.

One Christian counselor told me he thought parental guilt was a bigger problem for Christian professional people than for any others. Just being a Christian creates certain concerns—about biblical standards and eternal questions—non-Christians don't have to wrestle with. When higher education is added to the mix of faith, Christian professionals seem to have an inherent need to ask why. They naturally search for explanations. And when their penchant for intensive introspection provides them no answers, they feel guilty for their lack of understanding.

Many hurting parents suffer bouts of guilt because they started their marriages with super-idealistic dreams about what a Christian family should be. They had an unspoken assumption that as long as they maintained the right kind of spiritual influence in their family life, they would never have any problems or disappointments with their children. When the children grew up and began to strain at the parental controls or even cast off the values and faith they had been taught, these parents blamed themselves, thinking, *We must have done something wrong or everything would have turned out perfectly.* Then, in sifting through the memories, they uncover a huge supply of false guilt.

A strong dose of consistent Christian family life is the most effective inoculation a young person can have against the influences of the world. But sometimes the treatment just doesn't take or the effects are delayed. In other cases, because of personality makeup or interpersonal chemistry, a son or daughter has a strong negative reaction to the parents' faith. Christian family life is not a perfect preventive medicine. Thinking it is can create a lot of false guilt.

With this discussion of false guilt, I don't mean to imply that false guilt, because it is unnecessary, is any less painful than real guilt. Whether the guilt is justified or not, the feeling is the same. And it weighs heavily on the hearts and minds of many hurting parents.

One of the most common parental responses to guilt, real or false, is self-pity. It is an easy trap to fall into, as Dick Manville testified: "When I felt the guiltiest, I would find myself wallowing in self-pity. I'd recognize it for what it was, but I'd argue with myself, saying, 'It really is this bad!'

Then I'd feel even guiltier for the self-pity because I knew that, too, was wrong."

We mentioned introspection a little earlier as a cause of false guilt. But this self-searching also can be a response to guilt. A parent whose son or daughter gets in trouble begins to feel guilty. The parent begins to conjure up memories in his or her mind to try to find some explanation for the child's behavior. He or she remembers something he feels guilty about and that increases the guilt feelings. Then the cycle starts over. Again and again it happens. Feelings of guilt, more introspection, more possible reason for guilt, more feelings of guilt, more introspection, more possible reason for guilt—it becomes a vicious whirlpool that sucks a parent deeper and deeper.

Another common defense mechanism of hurting parents who feel guilty is to attempt to transmit some of that guilt to the child by our direct accusations or by acting the martyr. We suffer guilt, but since we realize we are not the only guilty parties, we try to create retaliatory guilt in the child who has hurt us.

A father told me how he did this. "My son Jim, who was living in another state, called to say he wanted to come home to live. So I gladly sent enough money to cover the expenses of the trip home and to pay off debts he had incurred during two years of irresponsible living. I was willing to pay any price to get Jim away from the influence of the friends where he'd been living. But sometime after Jim got home, when he asked about a European vacation my wife and I had been planning for years, I said, "We can't afford that now. Where did you think we got the money we sent you to come home?"

"I knew the minute I said that I'd made a mistake. Jim defensively snapped back at me with bitterness he'd never shown before or since. The resulting strain on our relationship took weeks to overcome."

When we try to impose guilt, we create real danger. As one young Christian who has caused her parents untold grief explained, "I had enough guilt of my own. If my parents had tried to heap any more on me, I would never have gone home."

If none of the common reactions to guilt are productive or healthy, then the question remains: How should a hurting parent deal with the guilt he or she feels? The answer depends in part on whether the guilt is false or justified.

The only effective means of dealing with the false guilt is to recognize and face it for exactly what it is. Sometimes it is difficult to separate the false guilt from the real guilt, but that needs to be done. One of the usual signs of false guilt is that it is hard to pin down. It fails to focus on any specific action that is biblically wrong; it is more likely to dwell on something that can't be changed.

False guilt needs no forgiveness, so there is no reason to confess it to God. It is better just to ask him to help you forget these feelings and get on with life. First John 3:18–20 suggests this strategy: "Let us not love with words or tongue but with actions and in truth. This then is how we know that we belong to the truth, and how we set our hearts at rest in his presence whenever our hearts condemn us. For God is greater than our hearts, and he knows everything." Hurting parents don't need to be paralyzed by false guilt; we are to get on with the business of loving and accepting our children.

Feelings of real guilt, unlike the false variety, do have a positive purpose. They call our attention to wrong. And they should not be discounted or ignored.

When we experience this kind of guilt, when we recognize our own sins and mistakes as parents, we need to ask God's forgiveness (and perhaps the forgiveness of our children) and then change our behavior. First John 1:9 offers another relevant promise: "If we confess our sins, he is faithful and just and will forgive us our sins and purify us from all unrighteousness." If we do confess our shortcomings and then continue to dwell on our guilt, we are really showing a lack of faith in God's forgiveness.

Guilt, whether false or real, is not something God wants us to live with as hurting Christian parents. Forgiveness is his concern—for us and for our children, and that is the subject of the next chapter.

SOMETHING TO THINK ABOUT

1. Make a list of five to ten common things you'd guess hurting parents might feel guilty about.

2. How would you define the differences between real and false guilt? Illustrate your answer with examples from hurting-parent situations.

3. Look up some biblical examples to see how different characters reacted to feelings of guilt.

CHAPTER 9

FORGIVENESS

For 'tis sweet to stammer one letter of the Eternal's language;
on earth it is called forgiveness.
— Longfellow

The supper leftovers were growing cold. But Alvin and Wilma Tomaszak still sat at the table talking when they heard the front door open and a familiar voice call, "Anybody home?" By the time they got to their feet, their youngest son, John, rushed into the kitchen to greet them both warmly.

"We weren't expecting you until late tonight," Wilma commented as she pulled out a chair and motioned John to a seat. "If you're hungry, I'll stick the leftover roast and potatoes in the microwave and you can eat in a minute."

"Thanks, Mom, that sounds good," John responded. "I finished my last paper for the term just after noon and decided to come home early. And I didn't stop to eat."

As John ate, the three of them talked, mostly about what had happened during the weeks since Alvin and Wilma had driven down to visit John at the university. The conversation stalled about the time John reached the end of his food. For a minute, he idly traced little lines in the gravy left on his plate. Then, without looking up, he said, "Mom, Dad, I've got a problem I don't know how to handle."

He seemed to fumble for the right words. "I don't really know how to tell you this." Both parents encouraged him, so John went on haltingly.

"It's something I've suspected for a long time," he said, "something I've known for the past couple of years." He stopped and swallowed. Both parents listened, somber but unsure what serious revelation John was about to make.

"I'm gay."

Those words flung a blanket of silence over the kitchen—a silence broken a few seconds later when the refrigerator kicked on with what seemed like a deafening roar. Both parents were paralyzed with disbelief. After an eternity, Alvin managed to mumble, "Are you sure?"

John took a deep breath, slowly looked up at his father, and nodded. "I'm sure."

With that, the silence settled again. John remained rooted to his chair, still drawing invisible patterns on his plate with his fork. He kept glancing up from time to time at one parent, then the other—waiting for some response.

When John made eye contact with his father, Alvin knew he had to say something. He could read pleas for reassurance and understanding in John's eyes. But he couldn't seem to muster any words for his son. Finally, Alvin tried to force conviction he didn't feel into his voice as he told John, "You're our son. And you'll always be our son. We love you, no matter what. But right now I don't know what else to say."

John nodded and managed a weak smile. "Maybe we can talk some tomorrow. I want you to understand."

Now it was Alvin's turn to nod feebly. Then John excused himself with an explanation that he had some errands to run and exited with a "good night."

Wilma fled to the bedroom, leaving the aftermath of supper on the kitchen table. Alvin followed her. Silently they undressed. And when they climbed into bed, the nightstand clock flashed 8:05.

For a time they lay side by side, as if bound and gagged by their emotions. Minutes passed before Wilma could manage an anguished sigh. "Why, Alvin, why?" Her emotions finally broke through and her body began to heave with sobs.

Alvin could offer no words of comfort or assurance, but he put his arms around his wife and held her close. All night long, tucked into the emotional protection of the fetal position, Wilma sobbed. All night long Alvin held his wife. His mind kept dredging up scenes from the past, comments John had made, things that had happened, little clues he should have seen, oddities that now made sense. Countless jigsaw pieces fell into place. But there were so many new questions to resolve.

"Why?" Alvin asked himself and God a thousand times that night. "Why this?" He could have understood anything else. But not this. It was impossible—beyond the realm of reality. And yet he knew he wasn't dreaming, because he couldn't get close to sleep.

Neither Alvin nor Wilma wanted to get up when dawn came. But the bed offered no comfort, so they rose and began the day. Neither of the Tomaszaks went to work that morning. They couldn't possibly have functioned.

At lunch John tried to talk again. Both parents listened as he told how he had been confused by his feelings since the seventh grade. He talked about his lack of interest in girls and the realization of his feelings of attraction for certain boys. He confessed being an active homosexual since he started college and had met a group of gays three years before. He admitted plaguing guilt about his homosexuality and told them a counselor had suggested it might help to confess to his parents.

When he finished, Alvin spoke. "But we still don't know why, John. What did we do that—"

"Nothing," John interrupted. "You're not at all responsible. I've asked myself why for years, but I still don't know the answer."

Alvin could hear the hurt in his son's choked voice. And he could see the regret on his face and in his eyes. Alvin was torn: part of him desperately wanted to hug his son and reassure him; part of him wanted to recoil in disgust from everything John had said. He compromised by once again sitting mute in response to John's confession. He had mouthed those reassuring words the night before, "You're still our son." But he couldn't even do that now.

Night came and again Alvin lay awake and held Wilma as she curled against him and cried. Again he mulled over John's words, his own feelings, and past scenes.

"About five o'clock in the morning it hit me," Alvin said. "I realized I never really thought about the sexual lives of my other older children. I saw them as my children and only incidentally as heterosexuals. But now I saw John as a homosexual whom I was stuck with as a son. I had let that little word *gay* turn everything upside down. I was looking at the sin instead of the son.

"When I separated the two, I could forgive John. And for the first time in thirty-six hours, a feeling of fatherly love burst loose in my heart. Forgiveness had given me the feelings to back up the empty words — he was my son no matter what."

Later that day Alvin shared his thinking and his forgiveness with John, and they began to rebuild an accepting, loving, and open relationship. Wilma also forgave and accepted John again.

John continued to struggle with deep bouts of guilt and depression. During one of these times, he called home for encouragement. He and his mother talked for a while before Wilma gently said, "You know, John, your guilt is just a natural reaction to sin. You can't get rid of the one without doing something about the other."

Soon after that John turned to God for forgiveness. He wasn't delivered from a homosexual orientation, but he is a nonpracticing homosexual and a Christian today. It couldn't have happened if he hadn't seen an example of God's loving forgiveness in the lives and actions of his parents.

Our relief from guilt we discussed in the last chapter is directly related to our own attitudes of forgiveness. God established the system that way; the Lord's Prayer confession "Forgive us our sins as we forgive those who have sinned against us" is only one of many biblical indications. So if we as guilty, hurting parents are going to experience God's forgiveness for our sins and mistakes, we also have to forgive the children who hurt us. And we should use God as a parental model for that forgiveness.

One of God's characteristics we need to consider is his *generosity*, his extravagant forgiveness. Not only are we assured that "if we confess our sins, he is faithful and just and will forgive us our sins," but forgiveness is available for the asking with no behavioral prerequisites. Even more impressive than that—God has given his forgiveness before we even ask for it. He takes the initiative; we only need to accept what he has already given.

Far from being extravagant, the tendency of many hurting parents is to be stingy with forgiveness. We say, "If he would just stop drinking and partying with that crowd he hangs out with, I could forgive him." Or, "If she just wouldn't argue with me when I ask her to go to church with the family, I'd forgive her lack of spiritual concern." We place behavioral conditions on our forgiveness.

The most common behavioral condition we impose is illustrated by the many parents who have said to me, "I'm ready to forgive. But he (or she) hasn't asked my forgiveness." We too often content ourselves with our inner feelings of forgiveness and load all the responsibility for reconciliation onto our children. But God doesn't do it that way. He holds out his forgiveness and waits for it to be accepted. If we are going to follow his example as a father, our forgiveness needs to be as aggressive and as obvious as our acceptance and our love.

As I talked with one hurting mother who realized the importance of God's style of forgiveness, she reached into her purse for her billfold and carefully extracted a well-worn paper, creased and yellowed. She unfolded it and handed it to me, explaining it was an anonymous prayer she had found years before and had prayed almost every day for her son.

The prayer read:

Merciful Father, I have been hurt by a certain person.
You know who I mean, God.
You know, too, I am struggling to keep bitterness and hate out of
    my heart,
        but it's so difficult to find the grace to forgive.
Will you help me, Lord?
I don't want to crowd these bad feelings into the dark corners of
    my mind;
        I don't want to deny the fact that I was hurt.
But I do want to forgive and get the hostility and anger out of my
    system at this very moment.
Perhaps someone somewhere is having a hard time forgiving me for
    something I said or did.
I might have hurt that person without ever knowing it.
So please, Lord, help me to forgive now.
It would be terrible to harbor ill-will against someone who might
    not even know he has hurt me.
So help me to forgive, Lord.

Another trait of God's forgiveness is that it is *all-encompassing.* The forgiveness is the same, no matter what the sin. Often as hurting parents we try to classify some sins as worse than others. We find it harder to forgive the "big" sins. Like Alvin Tomaszak, we say to ourselves, "Anything but this!"

We need to remind ourselves that while it is true that some sins present more serious immediate implications, the ultimate consequence of all sin is the same. Stealing a car is no more a sin than an untruthful excuse for a missed curfew. Sexual promiscuity is no more sinful than harboring a critical spirit. Yet we often let the "big sins" overwhelm us. Like the Tomaszaks, we confuse the sin with the sinner son or daughter. We let the "serious sins," such as drugs, homosexual behavior, or promiscuity color our whole view of our children. God doesn't do that. His forgiveness is broad enough to cover anything. He sees and loves the person underneath the sin. That is the kind of forgiveness we, too, should practice.

How do we as imperfect hurting Christian parents exhibit God's brand of forgiveness? I have gathered a number of clues from the parents who have shared for this book.

I think the first step is to recognize that forgiveness starts, not as an emotion, but as a deliberate act of the will. Many hurting parents are looking and waiting for a relieved, comfortable "everything may turn out all right anyway" feeling. But that is not forgiveness.

One father who understood real forgiveness told me about his son who had just been arrested and arraigned on a felony charge. "David told us he was guilty," this man said. "We have no idea what will happen when he goes to trial. The publicity has already humiliated our whole family. But my wife and I have determined to show our love and forgiveness to David. We only pray this will help him come to the Lord for his forgiveness."

This father and mother understood real forgiveness as a deliberate, conscious choice that says, "Nothing is going to stand between us, not even this." And we can make that choice long before we know how things are going to turn out.

Another requirement for total forgiveness is *a willingness to accept our share of the responsibility.* We can't completely forgive a son or daughter who has hurt us without admitting our own wrongs. Every broken or damaged relationship has two sides. If we are unable to accept our share of the blame, we are placing too much guilt on our children, and that isn't being forgiving.

We already talked about the guilt we experience as hurting parents. The preceding chapter pointed out the importance of seeking God's forgiveness. But that may not be enough. If we are going to be totally forgiving and accept our share of the responsibility in our relationship with our children, we may have to seek their forgiveness as well as God's. It is not easy to ask rebellious children to forgive the mistakes we have made as parents; such confessions are hard on our pride. But numerous hurting parents have told me how they had to ask forgiveness before they could see their way clear to fully forgive their children.

Like the healing strategies discussed earlier—acceptance and unconditional love—forgiveness needs to be *shown obviously* by hurting parents. In fact, acceptance and unconditional love are two good indications of forgiveness. All three attitudes are inseparably intertwined.

Often, showing forgiveness means voicing it. One father shared this example: "One afternoon just recently I was working outside my store when a car pulled up and my nineteen-year-old son, Blake, climbed out. I grinned and walked over to greet him, but when I saw who was driving, I froze inside. I only managed a semi-courteous 'Hi, Judy. How are you?' to the pretty young divorcée I knew Blake had been seeing for months—even before she had been divorced.

"A little while later, after Blake and I had closed the store and we were on our way home in the car, I said, 'Blake, I'm not going to harp and preach or criticize you for your relationship with Judy. And there's no need for me to hide the fact I'm hurt. You could see that tonight and you've known it before. But I want you to know I love you and I forgive you. And I want you to know I'm available. I want to be able to talk to you about any facet of your relationship with Judy and your feelings for her.'

"Blake smiled and said to me, 'Dad, I was hoping you'd feel that way. I kinda thought you would.'

"And since that conversation, I've never felt more at peace personally about my relationship with Blake. There's been an openness between us like we haven't had for a long time. And I feel more forgiveness than ever now that I've expressed it."

Despite this father's testimony to the power of spoken forgiveness, our words aren't always enough. Sometimes the real proof of our forgiveness lies in our actions.

When our son Mark returned home from his Florida stay, we wanted so much to express our forgiveness. We saw a way when he told us he wanted to get some experience in the construction and carpentry business. We bought an old house where Mark and his father worked for two years, remodeling it into beautiful apartments. Not only did that decision serve as a means of showing our forgiveness and love, but it opened the door for a family business partnership that enabled us to rebuild and maintain a close natural relationship with Mark during those difficult years.

Forgiveness, when it is obviously shown in words and deeds, has a way of opening the door on new opportunities of relationship. My husband and I found this true, and so have many other parents.

There is another step to total forgiveness, and that is *forgetting*; for many parents this seems to be the hardest. They can make the conscious decision to be forgiving, assume their own responsibility and ask forgiveness of their children, and even show their forgiveness with words and deeds of loving, accepting forgiveness. But they never can quite forget the hurt they have felt. Every time a new crisis comes along in their relationship with their child, they hash over past hurts and resurrect old feelings they thought were dead.

One father who illustrated this said, "Our money paid for the semesters of school she flunked. Our money paid the plane fare home when her boyfriend deserted her in France. Our money paid a doctor bill when she returned home sick. So every time she hints at needing a little cash, these memories keep coming back and I want to blurt out, 'You've squandered enough in riotous living.'"

A number of people with whom I have talked have failed to see the importance of this forgetting aspect of forgiveness. Usually, it is someone with no experience of parental hurt who asks, "Shouldn't a child know how a person feels, how deeply a parent hurts?"

I have to say no. Guilt is always a separator. Children will only recoil further from it and us if we try to arouse it. I think if we experience real forgiveness, we will lose all desire to tell a child how he or she has hurt us. And I have seen from my experience as well as others' that God will equip us with that kind of forgetful forgiveness if we ask him.

Total forgiveness requires one last measure from the hurting parent. He or she must take all these steps we have just covered — the forgetting, the showing, the accepting responsibility, and the conscious willing to forgive — and apply them all to every party involved. Our children may not be the only ones in need of our forgiveness.

I had a struggle with this in regard to some of my son's friends I felt were bad influences. I harbored a feeling of bitterness and disdain toward those boys for a time. But one day that "Forgive us our trespasses as we forgive those who trespass against us" section of the Lord's Prayer opened my heart. I realized I couldn't blame others for Mark's choices. I actually willed to forgive his friends, and the Lord flooded me with forgiveness and love for them.

Even harder for hurting parents to forgive than "undesirable" friends are sons-in-law and daughters-in-law when a child's marriage comes apart. "My son's wife took everything," one mother told me. "All the wedding gifts. All the furniture. She didn't even leave enough to furnish a skimpy one-room apartment. Before she left she ran up hundreds of dollars of bills unknown to my son in what seemed like deliberately planned bleeding. And on top of all that, she took off with our little grandson.

"The forgiveness came hard," she said. "I had to ask God for help, because I hurt too much for my boy to forgive her by myself."

Sometimes we may even have to find it in our hearts to forgive other Christians for their wrong attitudes toward us and our children. One man gave me this example: "I was thrilled when my son's friend became a Christian; I so hoped he could have an influence on my son, George. But my excitement was short-lived. The Christian mother of this other boy ordered her son to quit associating with George. And this boy not only quit coming to our house; he stopped speaking to my son.

"One day not long after that, George said to me, 'If that's Christianity, I don't want anything to do with it!' It took me a long time to work through my resentment toward that mother."

There may be times like this when we are going to have to forgive those people who are judgmental or vindictive toward our children. That is part of total forgiveness.

Often hurting parents need to forgive their spouses. I have had many hurting parents tell me they struggled with the temptation to blame each other for the problems with their children. Especially is this true when there is a basic philosophical difference in attitudes toward discipline. ("She's too strict and demanding," or "He's too lenient and he's never home when a crisis arises.") Resentments can spring up and grow. Those hard feelings can only be weeded out with a generous treatment of forgiveness.

We talked about the dangers of false guilt in chapter 8. But the subject bears mentioning again here, because it is impossible to totally forgive anyone else if we can't forgive ourselves. Self-condemnation will crop up in an unforgiving attitude toward others, so we have to apply the steps of forgiveness to ourselves as well as to others.

But there is one other party hurting Christian parents need to be sure they forgive — and that is God. The idea of forgiving God may sound a little strange at first, but let me illustrate.

I have a friend who has been a respected high school counselor with a meaningful ministry to hundreds of young people through the years. Hers was always a close Christian family with no serious problems, family feuds, or explosions of conflict as the children grew up. She couldn't understand when her oldest son came home from university to tell his parents he no longer believed in their God and began living an obviously non-Christian lifestyle that embarrassed them. She confronted God with accusing questions: "Why does this happen to us? Look at our neighbors! They don't even seem to care how their kids turn out. So why do you do this to us?" Her resentment toward God interfered with her relationship

with her son until she reached the point where she could absolve God of
any blame.

When we react to our hurt with angry questions of "Why?" to God,
we imply that he is somehow at least partially guilty of treating us wrong.
Of course, God has done no wrong. He doesn't need our forgiveness.
But we need to release him from any blame if we are going to be totally
forgiving.

We can't possibly overestimate the power of forgiveness. Every
human heart has a longing for it. The appealing attraction of loving,
accepting forgiveness draws every sinner toward the open arms of our
heavenly Father. The same kind of forgiveness will draw our sons and
daughters back to us and to faith in him.

SOMETHING TO THINK ABOUT

1. What do you think would be the hardest sins for a hurting parent to
   forgive in a child? Why?

2. Do a brief topical Bible study on the topic of forgiveness. What are
   some of the biblical characteristics of forgiveness you think are particularly applicable to hurting parents?

3. What is meant by saying hurting parents sometimes need to forgive
   God? Do you agree or disagree? Explain.

4. What is the best advice you could give to a hurting parent about the
   importance and necessity of forgiveness? How do you practice forgiveness when you don't feel forgiving or when the other party doesn't
   ask for forgiveness?

CHAPTER 10

DESPAIR

A man's spirit will endure sickness;
but a broken spirit who can bear?
—Proverbs 18:14 RSV

Emily Dreiser always looked forward to the times her daughter, Janis, stopped by home for supper. It only happened a couple of times a week since Janis had graduated from high school a few months before and moved into an apartment with two girlfriends. For Emily, letting go was hard. She missed the long talks at Janis's bedside, the honest, open sharing they had always had, the vicarious involvement she had felt in her young daughter's life. Janis had always craved her mother's attention and affirmation, and Emily had generously given it. But the relationship was different now, and Emily longed for the past.

Emily also felt great concern for her daughter's future. Janis had been dating Frank for several months. And while Emily didn't know much about him, she did know Frank wasn't a Christian. What little religious background he had was from another faith.

A number of times, Emily tried to talk about the importance of the spiritual side of a dating relationship. And as Janis seemed more and more enamored with Frank, Emily tried to reinforce the importance of Christian marriage in Janis's mind. It was a value that had been taught and emphasized in their home since Janis was a small girl.

One afternoon Janis stopped at home for supper after a shopping trip. As she came in and set her purse on the table, she placed a small bottle beside it. Emily, looking at the bottle, asked, "What's this, dear?"

Janis replied matter-of-factly, "It's special jeweler's cleaner to keep my diamond shiny and clean." She turned and held out her hand to show her mother an engagement ring.

"Here was my daughter trying to restrain her feelings. But she was obviously excited and wanted me to share or at least acknowledge her joy," Emily said. "But all I could say was a coldly polite, 'That's nice.' I saw her decision as a deliberate rejection of all the Christian values we had taught her."

Emily staggered through the next few days, burdened with concern. Each day the load of grief grew heavier until Emily determined one night to assault heaven with her prayers until she got an answer from God.

She started her prayer time by trying to find some portion of Scripture that spoke to her situation with Janis. She finally settled on the story of the prodigal son, but that gave no comfort, no direction to her prayers, because she couldn't accept the fact that Janis would have to leave home and hit bottom before there was any resolution.

As she continued to pray, Emily pulled out a hymnbook and began to read the lyrics, searching for some assurance from God. After turning page after page, Emily found a verse in a seventeenth-century song by Johann Friedrich Zihn that seemed to speak directly to her:

> *God liveth still!*
> *Soul despair not, fear no ill!*
> *He who gives the clouds their measure,*
> *Stretching out the heavens alone;*
> *He who stores the earth with treasure,*
> *Is not far from every one,*
> *God in the hour of need defendeth*
> *Him whose heart in love ascendeth.*

> *Wherefore, then, my soul, despair?*
> *God still lives who heareth prayer.*

Another verse concluded:

> *Yet will God keep safe and surely*
> *Those who trust in him securely.*
> *Wherefore, then, my soul, despair?*
> *God still lives who heareth prayer.*

This was just the reassurance she needed. God was hearing her prayers. He was almighty Master of the universe. Emily almost laughed with relief. What could one little eighteen-year-old girl do without the permission of the Almighty?

Emily got up from that prayer time with a freedom she hadn't felt for weeks. The worry was gone. She claimed and believed the promise that God was in control; he wouldn't let Janis marry Frank. In fact, two days later, when she chanced upon a friend who said, "I hear Janis is getting married," Emily replied, "She thinks she is."

One day shortly after that, Janis came home for supper. She asked if Emily would make the wedding announcement in the local paper. Emily told her no, saying, "You'll have to do that yourself." The next week the paper carried the announcement.

Emily's faith in God's sovereignty held fast through these weeks. But that did little to relieve the emotional hurt. She had always felt so close to Janis. And despite the assurance Emily had that the wedding would never come off, just knowing Janis planned to marry against her parents' wishes made Emily feel totally rejected.

"Like any mother, I so badly wanted to get involved and share this most exciting time in my daughter's life," Emily said. "I would even think of little gifts that would have been so practical to get her. But I checked my motherly impulses because I refused to condone this wedding. I would have no more considered helping Janis leap off a cliff.

"Time after time Janis tried to talk to me about her wedding—trying to draw me into the plans. But the ambivalent feelings warring inside me brought my emotions so close to the surface I couldn't calmly discuss the subject. The night she asked me my opinions on bridesmaid materials, I couldn't even speak; I rushed out of the room before I burst into tears.

"Gradually as the days passed, Janis talked less and less about the wedding in my presence; she just gave up. And the distance between us grew. I had to salve the hurt with the assurance I desperately clung to—that God was in control and wouldn't let the marriage happen."

The scheduled wedding was only a month away when it came time for the Dreiser family to move to another state. Emily and her husband tried to talk Janis into going and living with the family for a while and getting married in their new community. They even tried to persuade her to start college somewhere the second semester. But when the rest of the family moved from Minnesota to Oklahoma after Christmas, Janis stayed behind, still intent on marriage.

Despite the anguish she felt leaving her daughter behind, Emily held to her hope. When the date at last arrived, Emily stayed at home, waiting and wondering, confident something was happening back in Minnesota that would alter the wedding plans. All day Emily waited near the phone, expecting it to ring any minute with good news. But the call never came. She went to bed that night with no word.

It wasn't until the next afternoon that the phone rang and Emily heard Janis saying, "Hello, Mother."

"Hi, honey," Emily responded, the anxiety evident in her voice. "Where are you?"

"We're in Chicago"—she paused—"on our honeymoon."

There was a long silence. "Her words cut into me like a death-stab," Emily said. "I couldn't bring myself to make any kind of response. I guess she must have gone on to tell me a little about the wedding. But I don't really remember saying anything before she finally said good-bye and hung up.

"In the length of one phone call, I'd lost my anchor hold on hope and sunk into the depths of despair," Emily said. "I saw a finality to the marriage I could no longer change or prevent."

But even harder for Emily to accept than her daughter's marriage was the blow to her own faith. She had been so certain the wedding wouldn't occur. "The foundation of my world had crumbled. My faith was shattered. For the first time in my life, I felt God had failed me," Emily confessed. "I'd been so sure of his promise to intervene that I felt utterly betrayed.

"Either I had been totally deceived into thinking God had promised to stop Janis's wedding, or God had lied. I could see only those two alternatives; either one devastated my lifelong faith in God. If he lied, then I could never trust him for anything again. But if I had deceived myself, why hadn't he shown me the truth? John 15 promises that the Holy Spirit will lead us into all truth. Why hadn't that worked? Did this mean that forty years of growing in grace had made me no better than a heathen at determining God's will?

"The questions continued to plague me and chip away at what was left of my faith—even after Janis and I were reconciled and I accepted the fact of her marriage.

"A dozen years have passed since the wedding, yet I cringe every time I hear some speaker talk about the importance of Christian teaching in the family. I always feel like such a failure. Those who claim faith is caught more than taught make me feel even worse; they question my example. The years spent carefully teaching and living a Christian example in front of my family seem completely wasted.

"I've thought many times about parents who have lost a son in war—how anguished and torn they must feel. But I couldn't see that being worse than this. At least they don't have to battle any guilt.

"When I watch the dedication of babies in church, the doubts grab me. I listen to young parents make a covenant with God, and I think, *They can't be any more sincere than Earl and I were. Our foremost desire was to see our children come to know the Lord and live lives of service to him. So,* I think, *what's the use?*

"We have a good relationship with Janis and her husband and their children today. I apologized long ago for the attitudes I had about their marriage. They still haven't turned to a life-changing faith in God, but I've come to the conclusion that if God is going to reach them, he's going to have to use someone else. I've failed as a parent. And there's nothing more I can do."

Despair. The dictionary defines it as a loss of confidence, an absence of expectation or hope. The word perfectly describes the reaction of Emily Dreiser and a surprising number of hurting Christian parents.

Despair becomes the logical outgrowth of any or all of the common negative reactions hurting Christian parents experience. Dwelling on attitudes of shame, rejection, anger, or guilt is as dangerous as clinging to a log in the upper Niagara River. Eventually those emotions will drag us over the precipice, and we'll plunge into despair.

But in addition to the negative emotions we have already discussed at length in earlier chapters, a number of feelings and circumstances commonly contribute to hurting parents' despondency. Emily Dreiser provided us with several examples.

The first big contributor is the sinking *sensation of helplessness and inadequacy.* In a sense, every parent wrestles with these feelings. Every other profession or trade in the world has a training system combining education, apprenticeship, and on-the-job training experience. But the most crucial, demanding job in the world, the nurture and development of the next generation of civilization, is left to amateurs who have to blunder through by trial and error. None of us is prepared for the task of parenthood. And when we feel we have failed, our inadequacies loom large in our minds.

Emily felt it. After twelve years of living with a sense of failure, she still contends there is nothing she can do. She feels so helpless she doesn't think God can use her.

Helplessness often results from a sense of distance — emotional or geographical. You could see this happening in Emily's case. The more rejected she felt, the more despondent she became. The factor of geographical distance was better articulated by a Midwestern father who received a phone call from California saying his daughter was in intensive care after having attempted suicide. "I couldn't have felt more helpless if I'd been bound, gagged, and transplanted to some remote corner of the universe. The distance limited my response to despairing worry."

Many parents have talked to me about their feelings of helplessness because their children were away at school or they lived in another city or state. Any distance from our children narrows our options in relating or reacting to them.

Another factor that adds to parental despair is the *gravity of a son's or daughter's actions*. The more serious the problem and the consequences, the greater the possibility of despair. Of course, every sin is serious and any sin can be forgiven, but when facing the long-range consequences, such as the illegitimate baby of an unwanted pregnancy, the broken health of an alcoholic or an addict, a ten-year jail sentence for armed robbery, or an unhappy marriage, a watching, hurting parent can slide into despair.

The *suddenness of an unexpected hurt* can trigger despair, as illustrated by one mother who wrote to me. "Just a couple of weeks ago I read *The Hurting Parent*," she wrote. "And as I read the list of hurts so many others had suffered, I felt sympathy and pity. But I couldn't help feeling a certain satisfaction that I had been spared such ordeals.

"Just a week ago last Sunday my husband and I sat in the sanctuary of our church and listened to the choir our only daughter directed. We were so proud of her, her husband, and their three young children.

"But the next evening my son-in-law burst into our house looking for our daughter. She had told him she was coming over to see me. But soon after she had left, another woman from our church arrived at his door to say her husband had just left her and said he was taking off with our daughter. I couldn't believe it, but as that awful evening went on, the shocking truth was confirmed.

"That night I envied those who were lying peacefully in the cemetery and wondered why I had been forced to live through this horrible experience. We tried to pray, but we felt abandoned by God himself."

That was true despair.

Parents who get *backed into a corner* with no easy way out are also prime candidates for dejection. One mother told me about a teenage daughter plagued with emotional problems who was in and out of trouble at school. One day a social worker called to inform the parents that the girl had been arrested for shoplifting, and to ask whether they wanted her thrown into jail or committed to a mental hospital.

"We didn't know if her emotional condition was the reason for the behavior or whether her continuous antisocial behavior was prompting the emotional problems," the mother admitted. "We were faced with the two horrible choices, and we couldn't be sure what would be best for our daughter. The situation was hopelessly discouraging. We finally had her committed for therapy. But we couldn't be sure we'd done the right thing."

Despair feeds on that kind of uncertainty, when we just don't know what to do.

But the root cause of despair for Emily Dreiser (and many other hurting parents) was her *disappointment with God*. She was convinced she had a promise from him. She had asked for his intervention, but God didn't act on her prayers.

A father who experienced a similar feeling said, "I always looked forward to the caring attitude and inspiration I received from the midweek prayer and Bible study at my church. But one night the pastor asked if people had something fresh and up-to-date to share about how God was working in their lives. One rather pious old lady stood to her feet and with much enthusiasm and tiresome detail told a trivial tale about misplacing some 'important' book and how she prayed and the Lord directed her right to the spot where it was. As I listened I had to ask myself, 'What kind of a God is this who cares about lost books and won't answer my prayers for the lost son I haven't heard from for months?'"

What happens when we pray for a son or daughter and God doesn't act? What do we do when there is no miracle? If we surrender to our feelings, we begin to doubt everything but our worries and our hopelessness. And before long, like Emily Dreiser, we fall victim to despair.

Time is another great discourager. Many of us, like Emily Dreiser, have hurt for years, and if we concentrate on the lack of resolution, we discover the longer we hurt, the weaker our grip on hope. Even if we hang on to our faith, the pull toward despair can grow stronger and stronger with the passage of each month and year.

Despair pulls even harder when we think we have reached a solution, or at least see major progress, only to have our renewed hopes dashed to pieces with a setback. One father shared a disheartening example.

"We finally had a grand and glorious answer to our years of prayers," he said. "Our son had a real and marvelous experience with the Lord. He was miraculously freed from drugs and even gave up the cigarette habit he'd had since he was fifteen. For the first time in years my wife and I felt joy in our lives. Our son shared his new faith by telling anyone who would listen what God had done for him.

"Then it happened. After six wonderful months, he started shooting heroin again. The faith that had stood us through seven years of his addiction was shaken to its core. 'Why, God?' we asked. 'How could you let this happen? Haven't we hurt enough?' It seemed God was mocking us. We could find no reason to hope again. We couldn't find God anywhere."

The last big factor contributing to Emily Dreiser's despair was a *sense of finality*. Once her daughter was married, there was absolutely nothing more Emily or God could do to change that fact. For other parents it may be an irrevocable action — from a loss of their child's virginity to an arrest that means a lifelong criminal record for their child. The typical feeling is, *Oh, no! He has ruined the rest of his life. It'll never be the same again.*

That kind of despair is dangerous to Christian parents and their children. As the son or daughter watches the erosion of the parents' hopes and faith, he or she begins to think, I must be worse than I thought. And the chance for change grows dimmer.

Despair is probably the most dangerous, most difficult to deal with emotion that plagues hurting Christian parents. Its cloud of darkness can deprive us of the light we need for our physical, emotional, and spiritual health. And its continued shadow can eventually cripple us in any one, or all three areas of our lives.

There are no simple solutions to despair. When I concluded a two-hour interview with Emily Dreiser, her description of those long years of despondency so permeated my spirit I didn't even feel like working on this book. I couldn't think of anything encouraging to say. I had no answer for her.

But as I have thought about that interview and as I have talked to other hurting parents who have felt swallowed up by overwhelming despair, I have come to realize this book must address this reaction. I still haven't come to any easy solutions. But the best answers I have found are shown in the experiences of the parents who share in the next chapter.

SOMETHING TO THINK ABOUT

1. What major factors contribute to a hurting parent's feelings of despair?

2. Which of these factors trouble you most? Give examples.

3. If you had been called to counsel Emily Dreiser, what might you have said to try to counter her feelings of despair?

4. Scan through the Psalms in search of expressions of despair. Which ones could describe the feelings of hurting parents?

CHAPTER 11

HOPE

But these things I plan won't happen right away.
Slowly, steadily, surely, the time approaches when the vision
will be fulfilled. If it seems slow, do not despair,
for these things will surely come to pass. Just be patient!
They will not be overdue a single day!
—Habakkuk 2:3 TLB

Those who knew him say there never was a sweeter, gentler little boy than Steve McAllister. Then one day in grade school he punched a bully in the mouth and began a wild, eventful career as a fighter. The years of careful, conscientious Christian teaching at home and Sunday school were thrown out with the first swing of his fists. "By fifth grade I was the worst discipline problem in the entire Philadelphia school system," Steve said. "I was meeting three times a week with a psychiatrist who couldn't figure out what caused the hostility."

Years passed. His parents, Ken and Gladys McAllister, continued their regular pattern of Christian living and training, and Steve was still loving and kind with his family. At school, however, Steve seemed a different person—constantly fighting and in trouble.

The McAllisters prayed that Steve would grow out of his hostile stage. But high school was worse. Steve tied in with a group of older boys and added drinking to his troublemaking. "Sometimes I felt as if I was in school more than Steve was," Gladys said. "Time after time I'd talk the principal into letting him come back after he had been expelled."

Despite his penchant for trouble, Steve graduated from high school at age sixteen. Then he joined the army and shipped out for Germany, where he soon earned a reputation as a rabble-rouser. He organized a white gang that established a running feud with the blacks in his battalion. "One night I was in town alone when eight black guys jumped me and beat me up," Steve said. "I dragged myself back to my barracks and stirred up my gang to retaliate. We waited till the middle of the night, armed ourselves with shovels and picks, sneaked over to the barracks of the guys who'd beaten me, and attacked them while they were asleep in their bunks.

"We had open racial warfare on our military base. The army tried to keep the trouble hushed up, but things got so bad, armed guards had to patrol the barracks at night to keep us from killing each other."

Back home, Gladys didn't know all the details, but she was anguished over Steve. "I started every morning by searching the Scriptures and committing the day, myself, and Steve to the Lord."

One morning the McAllisters received a disturbing telegram telling them Steve was in critical condition after a near fatal car wreck. But that very day, before she could make the right contacts to get details from Europe, Gladys found a verse of assurance that said, "Behold, I am with thee, and will keep thee in all places whither thou goest, and will bring thee again into this land" (Gen. 28:15 KJV).

"And that," said Gladys, "was the verse I claimed for Steve the rest of the time he was in the service."

When Steve did come home from the army, his parents hardly recognized the person he'd become. His experience in Germany had hardened and embittered him until he chafed at any authority. He bought a motorcycle and started hanging out with a gang called the Vagabonds.

His parents didn't know the extent of Steve's involvement in gangland crime, drugs, and warfare. They could only suspect the worst when

Steve, wild-eyed, dirty, and belligerent, would come home for a couple of days to hide and recover from his latest fight.

Yet Gladys never quit praying for her son. "I clung to the verse that says, 'I know whom I have believed, and am persuaded that he is able to keep that which I have committed unto him against that day' [2 Tim. 1:12 KJV].

"It was the hardest to hope when I'd wake up in the night from a horrible dream. Satan would start slipping into my thoughts, reminding me of some of the dreadful things that had almost killed Steve and saying, 'There's nothing you can do. Steve will never make it.'

"Many nights I had to lift up my arms and ask forgiveness for holding on and ask God to take Steve into his hands. The only way I found to guard against the despair was to draw on the Scriptures. 'God hath not given us the spirit of fear; but of power, and of love, and of a sound mind' [2 Tim. 1:7 KJV], and '[He] is able to do exceeding abundantly above all that we ask or think, according to the power that worketh in us' [Eph. 3:20 KJV] were two verses I memorized."

Steve said, "I severed most of my contact with my parents because I didn't want to cause them undue worry. But Mom always seemed to know. Many times when I'd be hanging on to life by a thread, she would be shaken out of a sleep to get down on her knees by her bed and pray for my protection.

"I can see now that God answered Mom's prayers many times. I remember late one night when I was breaking into an apartment by climbing in a back window, someone inside pulled the trigger on a twelve-gauge shotgun and blew the window to bits. I felt the buckshot part my hair, but I wasn't even scratched. Even then I was struck by the memory of that Bible verse, 'There shall not an hair of your head perish' [Luke 21:18 KJV].

"Another time God saved my life when my girlfriend and I were riding my motorcycle down the highway. The engine began to sputter and lose power, so I leaned to the side to switch on the auxiliary gas tank when a big tractor-trailer rig plowed into us from behind. But because I had shifted my weight to the side just before impact, we were thrown clear of the wheels that mangled the bike."

But Ken and Gladys McAllister were seldom in a position to see God working in Steve's life. They usually saw the low points—like the times Ken went to jail to bail Steve out or the time they were called to the hospital to visit their critically injured son after the semi hit him. Steve couldn't walk for weeks after that motorcycle accident. So when the hospital released him, Ken and Gladys took him back into their home to care for him.

"Every night I would go to Steve's bedroom door," Gladys remembered. "And I would feel so torn. I wanted so badly to go in and sit on the side of the bed and say, 'Steve can't you see what's happening to you—what your sins are doing to you?' I so wanted to preach at him because the answer was so plain.

"But God wouldn't let me do it. I knew as long as Steve had that spark of rebellion in his eyes it was no use. So every night I stopped outside his door. Instead of going in, I stood there and prayed. Then I'd go to my own room and pray some more. Prayers and love were all I could give him—all he'd take right then. The rest was up to God."

Yet it must have seemed God wasn't making much progress either, because Steve went right back to his gang. He reestablished his leadership by going to a big rumble with another gang while still on crutches. A short while later, when Ken and Gladys went ahead with a planned move to Arizona, Steve stayed behind in Philadelphia.

Months passed and life became more and more dangerous for Steve. "I never even took a shower without wrapping my gun in a plastic bag and putting it in the soap dish. The cops wanted me. The other gangs wanted me. Even the mafia wanted me," Steve said.

"One night, after I'd heard there was a contract out on me, I told my friends, 'I'm going down to the 7-Eleven for cigarettes,' and I never went back. I disappeared and headed for Arizona."

For the first time in years, Steve lived without a gun. He even decided to enroll in a junior college. His parents were thrilled. But then an old gang friend discovered where Steve lived and showed up for help with five police cars screaming in pursuit. The friend was arrested, and Steve bailed him out. "But since the cops had his truck and it was stuffed with drugs, we knew we had to split before they found the stash," Steve said, "so we both headed back to Philadelphia."

Again Steve lived a life that rivaled the wildest crime movie. Once he and three friends with shotguns held off a gang of thirty motorcyclists who were bent on killing Steve. After he stuck the barrel of a gun in the mouth of a rival gang leader and threatened to kill him, Steve himself was beaten and left for dead by twenty members of that man's gang. For the next year and a half Steve carried a submachine gun slung over his shoulder and wore an old poncho blanket to hide it. His life became a nightmare of fear and violence.

In one drunken brawl he pulled a pistol trigger at pointblank range. The gun went off and blew the crotch out of the other man's jeans; but incredibly, the bullet didn't touch him.

Another time Steve waited inside an enemy's empty apartment, shotgun aimed at the door, ready to blow the guy away the moment the door opened. The man came home and was turning the key in the lock when someone called to him from down the hall; Steve's intended victim walked away and never came back. Time and again God protected Steve from committing murder. And despite all the trouble he was in, Steve was never convicted of a felony. His record remained amazingly clean.

When things got too hot, Steve disappeared for his health again and went back to Arizona. He enrolled in school the second time, with a secret ambition to become a lawyer and discover less dangerous ways to get around the law. This second start in college brought renewed hope to Ken and Gladys McAllister. "I prayed harder than ever," Gladys said, "especially that he would find a good Christian friend."

Instead, the one person on his campus Steve found he could relate to was John, another ex-military man—a fellow about his own age. John had taught martial arts to army special forces and had become a Zen Buddhist in the course of his training in the Orient. "I was fascinated with him," Steve said. "He was the most dangerous man I'd ever met, a fourth-degree black belt in judo, a master of other martial arts, an expert in deadly violence. Yet John seemed to have a calm, a control I envied.

"We became friends, and I began to take lessons from him. He taught me karate, and we talked a lot about truth and religion. And the more I learned about Zen, the more I longed for the kind of peace and contentment I read on John's face. I could see so many parallels between his life and the faith of my parents.

"After years of fighting and hatred, I realized I wanted something different. Something was happening inside of me. One day when I was home, I said to my mother, 'Mom, I'm coming back to God.'"

Gladys was overjoyed to hear her son mention God. "That's wonderful, Steve!" she exclaimed. But not wanting to pressure him, she let the conversation pass.

"That night as I prayed," she said, "I thought about Steve's words. Something about the way he said them made me wonder if he'd stumbled into some false religion. So I prayed he would find the real Truth.

"The next day at noon he called from school. He said, 'I meant what I said yesterday, Mom. I'm coming back to God.'

"So I came right out and asked him, 'You're not getting into any false religion are you, Steve?' He said he wasn't, but he didn't answer with very much conviction. So I told him, 'I just want to say one thing, Steve. There's only one way to come to the Father, and that's through the Son. You can't get to God without Jesus Christ.' He said he knew that and he had to go because his lunch hour was over."

That same night, Steve McAllister woke up after midnight and couldn't go back to sleep. He got up, drove to a nearby lake, found a place to sit on a big rock, and began to meditate. Using the control techniques

John had taught him, he tried to make his mind as calm as the surface of the quiet lake.

"As I sat on that rock," Steve said, "I thought about my life and compared it to John's and my parents'. They had what I wanted. Yet I remembered my mom's words, 'The only way to the Father is through the Son.' And as I weighed those words, I realized either Christianity was true and Zen Buddhism was false, or Zen was true and Christianity was false. Suddenly I really believed Jesus Christ was the Son of God. I knew my parents' faith was real because their love was real. And the instant that thought hit me, I fell off that rock and began to weep uncontrollably as I asked God to forgive all my sins. There, in the darkness, all alone beside that lake, I gave myself to God and felt him come into my life."

Early the next morning, after a sleepless night, Steve knocked on the kitchen door of his parents' house. When Gladys opened the door, he asked if she would fix him something to eat. She responded, "You know I will, honey."

As she fixed breakfast, Steve started talking. When he got to the part about the rock on the lake, Gladys McAllister put down her spatula and began to weep for joy. She rushed across the kitchen and hugged her son. Then Steve began to cry and they wept together.

"I can't describe the feelings that welled through me," Gladys said. "No one has ever experienced more complete joy. After ten long years of praying and hurting since Steve left for the service, all my hopes came true, all my faith was rewarded."

When her husband came home a little later that day, she told him about Steve. Ken was skeptical at first. Steve's friends were more than skeptical; they took up a collection for psychiatric treatment. But Gladys knew from the start that it was real. "God confirmed it in my heart," she said. "My son had finally found his Father and come home."

(Six years had passed between the night Steve McAllister found God and the time I interviewed his mother. During that time he had become a respected and successful businessman in his city. He was an active layman in his church and had a wonderful young family.)

Very few hurting Christian parents are subjected to as dramatic and climactic a struggle with a son or daughter as the McAllisters endured. But this story powerfully illustrates more reasons for hope than any other example I came across in my original research for this book. And these lessons of hope, these assurances that can be drawn from the McAllisters' experiences, are the strongest arguments I have found against the despair discussed in the preceding chapter.

The first assurance that should be especially heartening when we begin to feel completely helpless as parents is this: God's ability to work in the lives of our children doesn't depend on our resources. In fact, just the opposite is true. God isn't completely free to work in a child's life until we let go of that child and leave him or her entirely in God's hands. Obviously Gladys McAllister realized this, because she talked about worrying in the night and having to hand Steve back over to the Lord's care.

A father illustrated this same principle of release with this story: "I came home from a long business trip to find my wife, Ginnie, terribly distressed about the latest behavior of our sixteen-year-old, Donnie. He'd been giving us trouble for years, arrested by police a couple of times, and always a discipline problem at school. It seems the night before my return, Ginnie had specifically instructed Donnie to be home by midnight and he hadn't come in until nearly dawn. She'd been up all night and was frustrated and angry. 'You have to do something with Donnie before you take another trip,' she said.

"I tried to calm her by talking and praying with her about Donnie. But we couldn't come to any answers. So we prayed again, crying and begging God to show us what to do. As we prayed, a Bible reference came to mind—1 Corinthians 5:4–5. That can't be right, I thought. But I looked it up to be sure. It said, 'As you meet together, and I meet with you in my spirit, by the power of our Lord Jesus present with us, you are to hand this man over to Satan for his body to be destroyed, so that his spirit may be saved in the Day of the Lord' (TEV).

"I tried to argue with God, 'I can't do that. I can't let go of my own son.' But God seemed to be telling me that I had to release him, to give up my total responsibility for him. So after about an hour of wrestling with this idea, I surrendered and told Ginnie what I thought God was saying to us. Ginnie said, 'It's okay with me. I can't do anything with him.' So we consciously made the decision we would release him right then — to the power of Satan and the protection of God.

"After supper that evening, Donnie asked if he and I could talk. We went up to his room, and he lay down across his bed and flipped off the light. I lay down on his brother's bed and listened as he began. For four hours solid he talked, confessing all the garbage he'd been involved in, all the details of many things I hadn't even suspected. Several times he stopped and said, 'I can't believe this. I don't know why I'm telling you all this, Dad.' But I knew it was because I had turned him loose just hours before. And God was already beginning to work in Donnie's life.

"That was not the end of our struggles with Donnie. But it was definitely the turning point. And I'm convinced that if Ginnie and I hadn't been willing to let go, Donnie wouldn't be a Christian today."

Something unexplainable happens when we build up enough faith or when we get desperate enough to release our children, to entrust them totally to God. This last qualification is important — entrusting them to God. I'm not meaning to suggest we coldly send our children packing for hell with a "they deserve it" attitude. As 1 Corinthians 5:4 says, we are to do the releasing in the right spirit, the loving spirit of Christ. This doesn't exempt us from further concern, but it lays the responsibility for change on God. It keeps us out of his way and frees us from worry and the need to manipulate. Releasing allows us to concentrate on the only requirements God places on us as hurting parents — forgiving, accepting, and loving our children.

The second argument against despair, the assurance for parents who anguish over seemingly hopeless circumstances, is that God can use anything. Steve McAllister provided a beautiful example when he said, "I became a Christian through the influence of Zen Buddhism and the Holy Spirit."

One mother told me about the despair she felt when her son began living with a girl. "I thought she was nothing but trash," she said. "But she committed her life to Christ, married my son, and became a tower of Christian strength in their marriage. Her loving influence is now the best hope I have for his salvation."

One woman who had three drug-addict sons (they all eventually gave up drugs and turned to Christ) wrote me this about one of them: "My son heard God speak to him at the worst party he was ever at in his life. Two days later he called Teen Challenge and became a resident of their program. God completely changed his life around, and he felt a call to the ministry. Today, three and a half years later, he's married to a beautiful Christian girl and going to Bible school!"

After hearing such stories from so many parents, I have reached the confidence-inspiring conclusion that there isn't a person or a situation in the whole world God can't use to work in the lives of our wandering children. Knowing that, I can relax and trust him to choose the best time and means.

For the parent who despairs because prayers aren't answered, because he or she can't see any change or progress, there is another assurance to be drawn from the McAllister story: whether we see him or not, God is there working all the time.

Psalm 139 should be very reassuring for us when it describes the omnipresence of God:

> This is too glorious, too wonderful to believe! I can *never* be lost
> to your Spirit! I can *never* get away from my God! If I go up to
> heaven, you are there; if I go down to the place of the dead, you

are there. If I ride the morning winds to the farthest oceans, even there your hand will guide me, your strength will support me. If I try to hide in the darkness, the night becomes light around me. For even darkness cannot hide from God; to you the night shines as bright as day. Darkness and light are both alike to you.... How precious it is, Lord, to realize that you are thinking about me constantly! I can't even count how many times a day your thoughts turn towards me. And when I waken in the morning, you are still thinking of me! (vv. 6–12, 17–18 TLB, italics in original).

We need to claim this Scripture for our children.

Just as Gladys McAllister had no idea how God was protecting and leading Steve until years later, we may not always see God's design being woven into the fabric of our children's lives. But if we have committed our sons and daughters to God and have covenanted with him to do our part, we can rest assured God will never stop weaving and working his message into their hearts.

That reminds me of a promise in Jeremiah 33:3 (KJV): "Call unto me, and I will answer thee, and show thee great and mighty things, which thou knowest not." A friend of mine calls these the secret operations of the Holy Spirit.

One dramatic bit of proof that God is always working occurred in the life of one young man who had reached the end of himself. After years of degenerate living and sampling a catalog of sinful lifestyles, he tried to take his life. One night, half a continent from home and his Christian parents, he stumbled into an all-night laundry, picked up the only piece of paper he could find, and scribbled out a suicide note. He tucked it in his pocket and went out to the parking lot. There he took a length of rubber hose he used for a tourniquet when he shot heroin, tied it around his neck, and hanged himself from the luggage rack of a parked car.

He woke up in a hospital emergency room, recovered, and eventually went home. A little over a year later, he came to a real and profound experience with the Lord. Shortly after that, he was sorting through some of his things when he happened upon that suicide note. He turned it over and found to his amazement he had written on a Christian tract about the prodigal son.

"That spoke to me," he said. "It told me that even at the lowest point in my life, I hadn't been able to escape God." To his parents it said, "God was there working all the time." God doesn't always make us wait to see the great and mighty things he is doing in the lives of our children. Sometimes he does allow glimpses of his workings to help bolster our faith.

After we had found our son, Mark, in Florida, we informed a family friend who lived near his motel and asked her to make contact with him. One Sunday morning she was praying when God seemed to say to her, "Go see Mark and invite him to dinner today. Do it now!"

She arose from prayer, hurried out to her car, and took a shortcut to his motel. As she passed a major intersection on her route, she was amazed to see Mark walking toward the highway. She quickly turned around and offered our very surprised son a ride.

"What are you doing here?" he asked.

"I was coming to invite you over for dinner today," she responded.

He told her he was on his way to the expressway to hitchhike north. He was heading home. So our friend drove him to the interstate and dropped him off to find another ride. When she called us later in the day, we were ecstatic to learn Mark was coming home. As she told us about her prayer that morning and said, "If I had been a few seconds earlier or later, I would never have seen him," we were even more thrilled to realize God was working in split-second timing.

For hurting parents there is a fourth assurance we can't afford to forget. When the years of concern and hurt drag on and on, and our hope begins to shrivel, we need to be reminded that God is oblivious to time. He isn't bound by the structure of our days and months and years. Intellectually we know that from his place in eternity, God sees forever past and forever future; yet we get impatient and frustrated in our limited perception of time. We forget every person's spiritual pilgrimage is a unique and unending process; we seem to feel more comfortable when we can set up checkpoints along the way.

We quote the verse, "Train up a child in the way he should go: and when he is old, he will not depart from it" (Prov. 22:6 KJV). But we think of old as meaning eighteen or twenty-one. We hate to think "old" may mean a lifetime.

After years of worry and frustration, one mother finally came to understand her son's spiritual wandering as part of the process God was using to work in her son's life.

"It was then," she said, "I could relax with the thought that I might never live to see my son's salvation. I didn't care any less, and my prayers never slackened in intensity. But God gave me the patience to relax and wait for his timing." After waiting twenty-seven years, she saw her son finally come to God.

In chapter 10 we talked about hurting parents who are forced to helplessly watch a son or daughter take some irrevocable action, and we acknowledged the awful sense of finality that prompts them to despair: "His life is ruined!" or "Doesn't she know what she's done?" For these parents there is another assurance.

Our Lord is the God of the second chance. He can and will take our sons and daughters wherever they are, whatever their sins, however poorly they have lived their lives, and give them a fresh start. Often God will help them salvage their past by building on and using those very experiences that have caused hurting parents so much pain.

Once more the McAllister story offers a good example. Steve's success as a self-employed businessman gives him the flexibility of time to work with delinquent street kids as a volunteer with a Christian youth organization. Not only has his past equipped him to understand and love young people who are facing the same struggles and temptations he faced as a gang member, but he has spoken many times to Christian women's groups to encourage hurting Christian mothers who may be feeling the same kind of hurt he caused.

Our God is a persistent God. Because He is eternal, He knows no finality. He never quits. Knowing that should give us enough faith and hope to keep us doing our part as Christian parents.

SOMETHING TO THINK ABOUT

1. Think about your own situation or that of a hurting parent close to you. How could the situation be worse? What reasons do you have to feel hope?

2. Scan through the Psalms and find expressions of hope.

3. Why do we find it hard to "release" our children?

4. Which of the points in this hope chapter seemed most encouraging to you? Explain.

CHAPTER 12

WAITING

Understand that it is the family spirit, the organic life of the house,
the silent power of a domestic godliness, working, as it does,
unconsciously and with sovereign effect—this is it which forms
your children to God. And, if this be wanting, all that you may
do beside, will be as likely to annoy and harden as to bless.

—Horace Bushnell, *Christian Nurture*

What is our part as hurting Christian parents? How do we go about restoring, redeeming, and rebuilding our relationships with sons and daughters who have rejected our faith or the Christian values we believe are so important? After seeing years of careful Christian nurture and training fail, what more can we do to influence our children for the Lord?

I don't claim to have all the answers. (That is why I haven't talked as much about theory as I have reported on experience—my own and that of scores of people who have shared their thinking, their wisdom, and their hurts.) As I have lived with this subject, however, and as I have talked to others, a few basic principles have surfaced again and again. Those guiding concepts have given structure to this book.

We have devoted entire chapters to fellowship, acceptance, unconditional love, and forgiveness, which add up to hope. We have used other chapters to examine the dangers of isolation/shame, rejection, anger, and guilt, which add up to despair. And throughout the book hurting Christian parents have witnessed to the impact of practical strategies, such as communication with other hurting parents, ministry to others, diligent prayer, and adherence to God's Word.

I suppose to some discouraged, hurting parents these principles don't seem specific enough. But I have intentionally avoided step-by-step solutions because every parent-child problem is so different that any blanket answers would have to be glib and simplistic.

Instead of specific solutions that could be applied to only a limited number of situations, I have tried to lay out a few basic guidelines that apply whatever the parental circumstances—whether a daughter quits going to church because she is bored with "hollow traditions" or whether a son decides to undergo a sex-change operation. The application can vary greatly, depending on the individual parent and child, but based on the many experiences of the hurting parents who have contributed to this book, those principles of fellowship, acceptance, unconditional love, and forgiveness are mandatory starting points for any successful solutions.

I have not meant to suggest by the order of the chapters any order of importance to the principles suggested. They are all equally essential and perhaps inseparable. No one of them is enough by itself. But combined, these tested attitudes of acceptance, forgiveness, and unconditional love have transformed countless hurting Christian families.

The best-known biblical practitioner of these principles is the father of the prodigal son. When Jesus told this parable, the father symbolized our heavenly Father, God. But on closer examination, the prodigal's parent serves as a powerful model for hurting human parents as well.

The prodigal's father understood the importance of all the principles we have discussed. He was willing to release his son, to let him go and trust for his return. His acceptance, his forgiveness, and his love were exemplary; he bestowed them all with generosity. But the most important lesson that hurting Christian parents must draw from this parable is best highlighted in a thought-provoking sermon of Helmut Thielicke, the noted German theologian-minister.

As Thielicke's sermon title "The Waiting Father" suggests, the most striking trait of the prodigal's father was his patience. He waited. He didn't go chasing after his son to drag him home. He didn't try to convince the boy of his foolishness or make the boy feel guilty. He just waited, living the kind of life, offering the kind of love, providing the kind of home that would eventually draw his son back.

Thielicke argues that it was not guilt or disgust with himself that showed the boy the way home.

No, it's the other way around; it was because the father and the father's house loomed up before his soul that he became disgusted with himself.... It was his father's influence from afar, a by-product of sudden realization of where he really belonged. So it was not because that far country made him sick that he turned back home. It was rather that the consciousness of home disgusted him with the far country, actually made him realize what estrangement and lostness are.

Waiting is tough work. It takes effort and a special kind of discipline, a discipline of confidence that Mrs. Charles E. Cowman wrote about in her devotional classic *Springs in the Valley*, in which I discovered some very appropriate advice for hurting parents just in time to share it with a mother who wrote me about a daughter who had run away from home with a boyfriend. Mrs. Cowman wrote:

> There are two golden days in the week, upon which and about which, I never worry—two carefree days, kept sacredly free from fear and apprehension. One of these days is yesterday.... It was mine. It is God's.
>
> And the other day that I do not worry about is tomorrow.... Its sun will rise in roseate splendor, or behind a mask of weeping clouds—but it will rise. Until then, the same Love and Patience that held yesterday holds tomorrow.
>
> Tomorrow is God's day! It will be mine!
>
> There is left for myself, then, but one day in the week— today....

O friends, it is when we willfully add the burdens of those two awful eternities—yesterday and tomorrow—such burdens as only the Mighty God can sustain—that we break down. It isn't the experience of today that drives men mad. It is the remorse for something that happened yesterday; the dread of what tomorrow may disclose.

These are God's days! Leave them with him! Tomorrow is God's secret—but today is yours to live.

I know from experience that a lot of those "todays" can seem very hard to wait through. But God gives hurting parents a wonderful promise in 2 Corinthians 12:9: "My grace is sufficient for you, for my power is made perfect in weakness."

I like to think of this as something I call "hurting grace." It's the grace and strength God gives us to go on each day in the face of our hurt, the strength we need to do the hard work of waiting.

But how do we as hurting Christian parents develop and cultivate this quality of hurting grace in ourselves and in our families? How do we acquire this power that will disillusion our own children with their far countries and start them journeying homeward? Can't we do more than just wait?

Henry Drummond suggests the answer in *The Greatest Thing in the World*. He compares it to the process of induction.

Put a piece of iron in the presence of an electrified body, and that piece of iron for a time becomes electrified. It is changed into a temporary magnet in the mere presence of a permanent magnet; as long as you leave the two side by side, they are both magnets alike. Remain side by side with Him who loved us, and gave Himself for us, and you, too, will become a permanent magnet, a permanently attractive force; and like Him you will draw all men (and all sons and daughters) unto you.... That is the inevitable effect of love. Any man who fulfills that cause must have that effect produced in him.

Our ultimate goal and strategy as hurting Christian parents, then, is not to draw our wandering children back by our own powers. We shouldn't think of ourselves as instruments of change but rather as changing instruments, growing closer and closer to our heavenly Father, taking on larger and larger measures of his magnetism.

A friend whose hurt I have shared summarized this beautifully when she said, "We're all so busy being parents. But what God really wants is for us to be his children." My friend is right.

As growing children we become more and more like our waiting heavenly Father. And it is only the mirrored image of his character — his acceptance, his forgiveness, his love — that will ever draw our prodigal children home to us and to him.

CHAPTER 13

STORM

The human heart is like a ship on a stormy sea
driven about by winds blowing from all four corners of heaven.
—Martin Luther

For thirty years now, through three editions and more than a quarter million copies, this book has ended with chapter 12: "Waiting." That always seemed appropriate for a number of reasons.

I have never presumed to be an expert promising easy answers or dispensing professional advice for mothers and fathers of prodigal children. I wrote this book as a hurting parent myself, to share what practical lessons and principles I'd learned from my own very personal trial-and-error experience with my son, Mark, and from those other mothers and fathers who opened their hearts and hurts to me—lessons and principles that I prayed could be of comfort and help to other hurting parents and their families.

The feedback I received through the years told me readers identified with me and my experience, and they appreciated this book principally because they knew I had walked, and was still walking, in their shoes. Indeed, any credibility I had to write on this subject was based on the fact that, like so many readers, I, too, was a hurting parent who was still "waiting."

However, on the occasion of this updated and expanded edition of this book, candor requires me to disclose the "rest of the story" that has taken place in our family in recent years.

First, let me assure you that through the many years of waiting, I tried never to presume to tell the Lord what he needed to say to Mark, how or when he should work in Mark's life, or what he ought to call my son to do. What I have frequently prayed has been, "Dear Lord, please penetrate Mark's thought pattern. Speak to his mind and his heart." From Mark's own testimony, which you are about to read, I think you will conclude that God certainly answered that prayer—and that God knew, much better than I ever could have known, the very best way to get through to my son and accomplish more than I might ever have dared to ask. Indeed, at the risk of ruining any suspense, let me just say that as an eighty-six-year-old widowed mother and grandmother today, I have found having my son Mark, his wife, Angela, and their four beautiful daughters as next-door neighbors to be a surprise blessing and one of my life's greatest joys.

But to bring you up to date as to how this all came about, I need to reset the stage by going back, almost to the beginning of this book where and when my husband, Ralph, and I suddenly found ourselves in the large fraternity of folks who are prodigals' parents.

As you already know, our son Mark eventually returned to Kentucky from Florida on his motorcycle. But there was at that point no joyous reunion, no fatted-calf celebration of his full restoration to the family.

Thankfully, there were many opportunities to display acceptance, forgiveness, and unconditional love to our son. And we took deliberate steps to insure regular interaction with Mark; as I have also told you, his father and I even purchased an old house he could remodel as a beginning for his own construction business.

Mark rented an apartment to live less than thirty minutes away in Lexington. However, despite his physical proximity, Mark remained in that "far country" spiritually. So we watched and prayed and waited.

For years! To what end?

I'll now let Mark relate that part of the story himself:

To tell "the rest of the story" my mother is referring to here, I, too, have to go back to the beginning and get a running start. The part you need to know about began on that eventful day Mom recounted in the opening chapter of this book.

It was a cool, crisp autumn morning in November. I was in my second year at the local, small Christian college where I was following in the footsteps of my dutiful older brother. But I'd had enough. I wanted to find out what life really had to offer — not this sheltered existence on a conservative college campus in my too-small hometown.

I revved the engine on my motorcycle. My blood was pumping. I leaned back against my duffel bag packed with camping gear, clothes, a few tools, and a paperback copy of Walt Whitman's *Leaves of Grass*. Drinking in that delicious moment, I popped the clutch and went through three gears before I banked left onto the street in front of the campus.

I was leaving! Leaving home and family. Leaving school — dropping out unannounced just weeks before the end of that fall term. Leaving my puny little hometown and all that it stood for. What could it offer compared to the real world?

Every cell in my body was on red alert. I was headed for independence. I was ready, to use a borrowed phrase, to suck the marrow out of life. I was nineteen, and I'd outgrown this place and its God.

I could taste freedom, I could smell it. And as I crested the last hill out of town, I could feel it rushing past my face in the wind — freedom!

My motorcycle and I headed south, because that's where the warmer weather was. It was months before my folks knew where I was at all. But after they found me, I began getting letters almost every day from my mom. And the lines of communication stayed open from then on.

After several more months, I rode my motorcycle back to Kentucky, but I didn't want to have anything to do with the church. I didn't want to have anything to do with God. That, you see, was for people like my folks, who needed it. I had graduated.

The world seemed full of options in the early seventies. I got involved in the construction trade and eventually became a framing contractor. All around central Kentucky I built houses, townhomes, apartment buildings, and horse barns. I even framed a church or two. Business was good. But something was missing.

Just a few days before I turned thirty, I married Angela. And for those in my baby boomer generation, turning thirty was a landmark event. We eloped because we weren't sure how to do the wedding. Angela grew up Catholic, and her family was looking for a big celebration of some sort that was going to be very different from my family's expectations. So we ran off to Tennessee to get married and then honeymooned in the Bahamas.

Business continued along pretty well for several years. Our first daughter was born, and we built a new riverfront home down in the Kentucky River gorge. We'd been married about seven years when I acknowledged that something was still missing in my life. Angela and I started talking about this sense of restlessness we both felt.

Maybe, if we just lived in the right place, with plenty of adventure and excitement, we wouldn't feel this way. So we started looking around, shopping for somewhere to move, a more interesting and exciting (and warmer) place to live and to work.

We found a little island in the Caribbean Sea called St. Croix — part of the U.S. Virgin Islands. Because this exotic tropical locale was under the U.S. flag, we wouldn't face any restrictions living and working there. So we sold most of what we had in Kentucky, packed the remainder of our personal possessions in a shipping container, and moved to the Caribbean in search of adventure and excitement.

That was in 1988. We'd been on the island for less than fifteen months when we ended up getting more adventure and excitement than we had bargained for. In mid-September 1989, Hurricane Hugo came churning across the Atlantic right toward our little piece of paradise.

Early Sunday evening, September 17, I glanced one last time around the yard, double-checking to make certain I'd stowed all the loose items — lawn furniture, toys — safely under the wooden porch deck. Having recently seen a video where another Caribbean hurricane had hurled coconuts like cannon balls, I decided to take no chances. With my machete I lopped all the fruit off the nearby palms and stored the coconuts safely inside the house.

By this time, the trees had begun to bob, some of them bending so much they touched the ground. From our perch atop a mountain ridge, I looked out over the ocean to the north, where on a clear day we could usually make out the islands of St. Thomas and St. John on the horizon. Visibility was already reduced. Low gray clouds raced overhead. Rain was promised. A half mile away I could see the usually tranquil and tropical blue ocean whipped into a frenzied mass of chaotic white caps.

For days now I had been getting ready for this storm. Monitoring it on the radio, plotting its course on one of the little maps they hand out for free at local grocery or hardware stores, watching how Hugo's track inched mile by mile across the Atlantic right toward us. This was our first experience with a hurricane, so I'd sought and followed the advice of longtime-islander friends. I'd bought sheets of heavy plywood, covered all our windows, nailed them up tight, even braced the plywood from the wooden deck. We laid in a supply of food, water, and enough other essentials to survive a week or two without power.

Most of our experienced friends didn't seem overly concerned. "Hurricanes can be a great excuse for a big party," they told us. "Just make sure you are with some fun-loving people when it hits, because you're not going to be able to get around for a while. Oh, there's a lot of rain and there's some wind, and at worst, some inconvenience and an unscheduled holiday."

But those friends had no more experience than we did dealing with anything like Hugo. For unbeknownst to any of us, what was bearing down on our little island was a monster storm, steadily growing and building to the point that the experts would rate it as a once-in-four-hundred-years hurricane.

Of course I had no way of knowing that as I made final preparations this Sunday evening. I moved our vehicles away from the trees where they were usually parked. I'd put tape across the windows in case anything hit them, so that the glass wouldn't shatter and blow but would be held in place. As dusk crept in early, the strengthening wind and our hilltop exposure made me uneasy — enough so to persuade me it was definitely time to go inside and wait.

The lights were still on when I entered the house. But our usual panorama, overlooking a lush valley sloping down to the island's beautiful north shore, had been replaced by the barren brown backside of the plywood covering our windows. Adding to the dreary, claustrophobic ambiance was the eerie, unsettling sound of the wind as it sought out, and whistled in through, every little crack and crevice — as if insisting there was more to come.

The phones, which on St. Croix were never very reliable, somehow remained operative until well after dark. Earlier in the day, we had called stateside to talk with friends and relatives, letting them know we were ready for the storm. Not to worry — we'd be out of touch for a while. From these folks with access to radar and weather reports, we'd also heard that Hurricane Hugo was still heading straight for us and gaining intensity.

Now, as first the phones and then the power cut out, the flickering flames of candles and kerosene lamps gave the darkened house an aura of exciting anticipation. We'd moved our two small daughters to the master bedroom in the concrete portion of the house. They were already asleep — three-year-old Frederica on our bed and six-month-old Ivey in her crib. But it was way too early and too noisy for Angela or me to think of retiring for the night.

At one point, Angela came into the bedroom to tell me she'd been reading the newspaper by candlelight at the dining room table when she thought she'd felt a mist—as if tiny particles of rain were blowing straight through the plywood I'd nailed over the sliding glass doors. Being a careful, experienced carpenter, I knew that would be impossible, but I immediately took the flashlight from Angela and headed into the dining room to investigate for myself.

When I shined the light through the sliding doors that normally led out onto our deck, I could see the back of the plywood flex in and out with every wind gust that hit the house. But the wood remained in place where I'd nailed it around the door frame, so I couldn't see where any water should be getting in through ... *What was that?*

I felt a mist on my forehead!

I shined the light up to where the ceiling and roof were attached to the wall. Not only could I see where the water was getting in, but I suddenly realized we had a more serious problem. The edge of the roof was rising up three and four inches each time a sledgehammer blast of wind pounded against the house and surged up under the eaves. I turned and raced back into the bedroom to tell Angela: "I need you to hold the light. I have to get some braces for the roof—or it's going to go!"

So it was that my wife held our six-month-old in one arm and pointed a flashlight with her other hand as I strapped on my nail apron and climbed up a hastily positioned step ladder. Fortunately, I had brought a few two-by-fours into the house before the storm hit. I could use them.

Once on the ladder, I could literally feel the impact of the winds slamming, then vibrating through, that outside wall. Each blow sent the roof lifting up three or four inches before settling back down on the top of that wall again. When my target wasn't moving, I drove nails through my 2x4s into the ceiling rafters. Then I scampered down the ladder and braced the roof by nailing the other end of the boards into the wooden frames around the dining room doors and windows.

I don't know that I had ever in my life felt so inadequate as I did in those desperate minutes, feeling the violence of those winds shake the house and watching the roof try to levitate as I fought to anchor it into something solid enough to withstand hurricane-force winds. Atop a short step ladder in that darkened dining room, it felt very much like it was "me against the world."

When I'd nailed in my last two-by-four and descended the ladder for the final time, I took the flashlight from Angela and walked into the very next room. There I shined the light up at that strategic point where ceiling meets wall, to see the roof lifting up and down in that room as well. Yet I had no more braces. There was nothing more I could do.

I told Angela, "It's only a matter of time before the roof goes! We need to get both girls into the bathroom right now." That was the one room in the house with a poured concrete wall all the way around. Because it was also the smallest room in the house, it seemed to me the safest, most enclosed place to be. So I dragged the crib mattress in on the bathroom floor for the girls, and we set a cooler full of bottled water and emergency snacks in the shower. We hadn't been in that bathroom fifteen minutes when we heard the first ripping sound as the wind began to tear the roof off the house.

Angela grabbed baby Ivey and jumped over me into the concrete-encased shower stall. And I was right behind her. With Frederica in one arm, I reached back out and snatched up the crib mattress, which I then jammed in over our heads. As Angela and I sat wedged together on the Coleman cooler, holding tight to the little ones on our laps, I could hear the popping sound of the braces I'd nailed into the rafters. Then came the deafening sound of tearing and splintering wood as section after section of the roof peeled away.

We shined the light out through the louvered shower door to see boards, ceiling, even chunks of concrete ripped from the walls crashing down on the bathroom floor where we'd been only moments before. Within minutes, two feet of debris covered the floor just outside the shower stall.

The whistling wind had transformed into a terrifying tempest that sounded like a herd of freight trains rumbling overhead. Rain began dripping down around the vinyl baby bed mattress I now held in place over our heads—the only barrier between us and one of the worst hurricanes in history raging through the darkness above and around us.

Suddenly, louder even than the wind, came a startlingly loud shatter. Angela jumped! "What was that?"

"Probably the mirror in the dining room," I told her. An even more terrifying sound followed as the wind wrenched the deck off the front of the house and with it the boarded-up frame of the sliding glass doors in the dining room. Crash followed crash, as one by one, all the windows on the ocean side of the house shattered from the inside.

It was as if God was blowing away every excuse that I'd ever given him. I had grown up in a Christian home, hearing and knowing about the Creator and Redeemer of the universe, and I, in my youthful arrogance, had said, "I don't need that."

But now, as the storm slowly but steadily twisted and tore our house down around us, my back pressed so hard against the concrete wall of that shower that I could feel the very pulse of that hurricane pounding against the other side of that wall, God gave me a glimpse of his truth. Sitting on that razor's edge of reality, I suddenly realized how insignificant I was, how foolish I'd been in holding him off and saying no to him. How much I needed him.

There in that three-by-three-foot shower stall, I admitted: "Lord, I haven't been honest with you; I haven't been honest with myself. I've made you in an image, far distant and removed, so that I could do what I wanted to do when I wanted to do it. How foolish of me! And now I can't do anything to protect my family."

So I began to pray. I didn't get too elaborate with my thoughts or my words. I kept trying to think of something ... anything else I could do ... somewhere safer we could go. I prayed repeatedly for wisdom to know what to do and the courage to do it. I envisioned God's hands around the house, protecting us and holding up the shower walls. And finally, I prayed that my wife and daughters would be spared. I was so uncertain I'd make it that I reminded Angela that if she was trapped in the shower after the storm, she could easily kick the slats out of the door and crawl out. Not that I'd given up all hope of survival, but I needed to be realistic.

As a builder I knew the integrity of any house's structure depends on the soundness of its bond beam. The friend who had rented us our home had told us she'd once had a fire. And in making my own plans to do some remodeling for her, I had found a number of weaknesses in the home's basic structure.

When I had envisioned the possibility of the roof blowing off, I'd known for certain what we should do: get into the bathroom. But now when I considered the possibility of the walls beginning to crumble in this battering-ram wind, I kept searching my mind for some safer place. Yet I could think of no recourse at all.

Sitting there trapped, cramped and helpless, time seemed to creep minute by minute. With each five minutes, ten minutes, especially each thirty minutes, I knew or at least hoped the storm was passing by—and I was grateful. Yet I wondered how any wind could blow so hard for so long. Ten o'clock. Eleven o'clock. Midnight. If anything, the storm seemed to grow worse.

We found out later the sustained winds eventually reached 165 miles per hour. Some of the gusts topped 200 miles per hour. And the reason it lasted so long was because the storm's forward progress slowed to between one and two miles per hour, meaning Hugo stood almost still for hours as it body-slammed St. Croix.

Sometime around 1:00 a.m. the winds suddenly ceased and everything became eerily quiet.

We wondered if it could finally be over. But in the calmness came the terrible thought, *This could just be the eye of the storm!*

Nevertheless, Angela and I took the opportunity to stand up and stretch our aching muscles for the first time in almost five hours. With our girls in our arms, we even stepped out of the shower into the debris-strewn bathroom for a very short time. But we didn't dare go farther for fear we were inside the eye wall and the storm might resume as quickly as it had stopped.

Indeed, that's exactly what happened — within minutes Hugo exploded again at full force. As the storm's roundhouse blow hit us from the south for the first time, it brought with it the sound of hail. At least we thought it was hail, until we realized the teardrops and slivers dripping down the shower walls around our vinyl mattress "shield" were not ice, but rather bits of glass churned up by the changing winds.

The upside of having been through the eye of a hurricane is that you then know approximately how long the second half of the storm is going to last. The downside in our case was the terrible realization that there would be another five and a half hours of stormy violence and destruction to come.

I started praying again, calling out to God, "Give us peace. Give us courage. Wrap your arms around this house." At some point, I began praying out loud, and it must have been very loud, because even above those freight train winds roaring again over and through the house, Angela leaned closer to me and wanted to know, "Are you praying?"

"Yes," I admitted. "Yes, I am." Angela told me later that when she heard that, she was more scared than ever. You see, she'd never before known me to pray.

We'd been married seven years, and she'd been trying to get me to go to church, because as a good Catholic, she knew now that we had children, we needed to get them proper spiritual training. But I said, no, I worked hard Monday through Saturday. Sunday was my one day for myself, to relax, spend time with family and friends, and play beach volleyball. I wasn't going to give up any of that. And I'd always been so adamant in my resistance to all things spiritual that Angela figured if I was praying, things must be even worse than she'd feared.

As Monday dawned, the walls still shook. The worst of the gusts seemed to be slacking off, but the storm remained too dangerous to venture out. So we stayed put.

Not until almost 8 that next morning did I finally risk a one-man reconnaissance out into Hugo's gradually slackening winds. The relief that came with the realization that we had all survived was quickly tempered by what I saw.

Some of our walls were still standing, but other entire rooms had totally blown apart. The living room was simply gone. And the majority of our remaining earthly possessions looked as if they'd been blenderized with equal parts glass, wood, assorted building materials, green bits of vegetation, and rainwater—creating an ugly, warm, soupy, smelly hurricane stew.

Stepping out into the yard proved even more depressing. What had been a lush tropical paradise the day before now resembled nuclear winter. The trees had been stripped of their leaves. And everywhere I looked down the mountain, trails of debris fanned out from cement pads and foundations where houses used to be. *Could we be the only people left alive on the entire island?* I wondered.

Using my machete, I whacked a trail through tangled brush and downed tree limbs in search of our nearest neighbor. He had survived with several dry rooms and offered us temporary refuge. So I headed back home to get Angela and the girls.

Before she set foot out of the shower stall, I warned my wife, "It's like the Holocaust out here." And it was. As I helped her climb over kitchen cabinets and wade through the ruined remnants of our physical belongings, we had to keep telling ourselves none of those things mattered. It was all just stuff. What did matter was that our family was alive and safe and together. We had survived! That was reason enough to be grateful.

But for me there was more. Walking out of the wreckage of our house with my family that Monday morning, I realized things could never be the same again. I had been given a great gift. This was the first day of a new life, with a renewed faith.

Over the next few days we salvaged what we could from the debris in and around our home. With almost no usable food, none to be purchased anywhere on St. Croix, and no relief supplies arriving for days, we bartered the use of our portable generator for meals with neighbors and friends. And on the sixth day after Hugo, having had no time yet to begin to process what all had happened to us, Angela and the girls flew back to the States to stay with relatives, while I stayed on to do what I could to rebuild the island.

Telling the builder-developer with whom I'd been working that I saw more important work to be done than replacing the roofs on the vacation homes of millionaires, I quit my job as a construction supervisor and volunteered my services to the Virgin Islands Assistant Commissioner of Health. And that is how, one week after Hugo, I found myself distributing emergency medical supplies for the island of St. Croix.

Six weeks after Hugo, Angela and the girls returned to the islands, and we moved into a small garage apartment I had found. For the next three months, we lived there without electricity. Five months passed before phone service was restored to our part of the island. But none of that really mattered much as I continued my work with the islands' Department of Health, helping coordinate the reconstruction of the island's only hospital, which provided most of the health services for the people of St. Croix.

Like our adopted island and so many of its people, we slowly worked through the challenge of recovery. We found a moderately damaged, but still structurally sound mountainside home that had been abandoned by stateside owners who had literally walked away from the storm mess and never come back—not even to clean out their refrigerator. We purchased the property in a buyer's market at a hurricane-sale price. And then we began the labor-intensive challenge of shoveling out, cleaning up, reroofing, and restoring our "new" home to a livable state.

Late one night, months after the hurricane, Angela and the girls had gone to bed while I stayed up for a little private devotion time. I read and meditated on two passages from Paul's epistles. In Romans 10 the apostle Paul, quoting an Old Testament passage from Isaiah 52, wrote, "How beautiful on the mountain are the feet of them that bring good news." I looked at my feet.

Then in 1 Corinthians 9:16 Paul exclaimed to his readers, "I am compelled to preach. Woe to me if I do not preach the gospel!"

Ever since the hurricane, I'd been working fifty to seventy hours a week for the U.S. Virgin Islands Health Department, starting as an unpaid volunteer, doing whatever I could to serve our many island neighbors left in such dire straits by Hugo's destruction. And I had discovered great satisfaction in that service, knowing I was making a difference in the lives of others after so many years of living life in pursuit of my own gain and adventure.

But as I sat reading my Bible all alone in the quiet that night, the images in those two passages seemed to collide in my thoughts as the still, small voice of the Holy Spirit said, "Mark, I want you to preach the gospel of the good news of Jesus Christ." And in an instant, I said, "Yes! Yes!"

It didn't take a two-by-four up the side of my head this time. It didn't take another hurricane. Sometimes God works and speaks through a mighty wind. But at other points in life, all that's required is a whispering in one's spirit. By this time, the Lord had my attention, and instead of running from him into a far country, I was following hard and fast after him. I could hear the call of God, and I was finally ready to say, "Yes!"

When I did, it was like a coming home—better than the best welcome-back party ever. I knew in that instant that this was the plan and the purpose God had for me all along. For thirty-seven years I'd followed many dead ends that the world promised would lead me to meaning and significance and purpose in life. Now suddenly I realized that God, as the Creator of all that is, and as the Redeemer of that creation, knows each of us better than we know ourselves. His plan was not just a good plan. No—it was the very best possible plan for *me*.

I saw all this very clearly that night when I finally said yes to God and his call. I was so excited to realize I had discovered the missing purpose and meaning of life I'd been searching after for so long, that I wanted to rush right into the bedroom, awaken my sleeping wife, and tell her what had just happened. But I wasn't at all sure how Angela would react. So I prayed fervently for the next two weeks, waiting and watching for just the right opportunity to present itself.

Finally, in the middle of the night, tossing and turning, too restless to sleep, I did awaken and inform Angela that I believed God was calling me into the ministry. Her immediate drowsy response shocked me. "Okay," she said, agreeably enough. "How do we do that? Where will we have to go?"

I didn't have any of the answers to those questions figured out yet. But heartened by her initial reaction, I assured her we could talk more in the morning, and then I fell peacefully asleep.

The bright light of the next day brought with it a complete change of heart in Angela. This was more like the reaction I'd feared. She had of course realized I had become a different person since the hurricane, and for the most part she had seemed pleased by the change. Yet I knew she hadn't fully understood what it meant, and now all her questions and doubts and wariness seemed to surface at once.

Angela told me she was glad I had found this faith, but this ministry idea wasn't what she'd signed up for when we got married. Why couldn't we just go to church on Sundays and come home like normal people — the way she'd been wanting us to do for years. Why did this have to change our whole life? We'd come so far, survived so much, and worked so hard to make a life on St. Croix. Now that things were beginning to look up, how could I expect her to give up our island dreams? This calling I'd felt might be my thing, but it wasn't hers. If I needed to go back to the States to finish college in order to prepare for some ministry God had for me, fine. But she informed me that she and the girls would be staying right there on St. Croix until I returned.

I knew there was no way that could happen. But I decided to drop the subject for a while and give Angela a little more time to accept the idea as I quietly began to explore and pray about what God would have me to do.

That's when Angela became pregnant again. And when she is pregnant, my strong and independent wife becomes physically and emotionally dependent on me in ways different from any other time in our lives. All talk of her staying alone on the island with the girls while I went back to study in the States immediately stopped. And within a few months we'd leased our house on St. Croix, packed up what few essential possessions we had left, and moved back to Kentucky.

After twenty years, my life had come full circle. And the irony certainly didn't escape me. I was giving up my dreams and a wonderful life in a tropical paradise to return to the same small town I'd been so desperate to escape two decades before. I was moving my family into one of the first small two-bedroom apartments I'd ever built, in the old house my parents had bought for me to remodel and give me my start in the construction business. I was enrolling again in the small Christian college I had dropped out of midterm to climb on my motorcycle and roar out of town in quest of freedom.

And I was now absolutely thrilled about the prospect of all of this!

Angela? Not so much so. This still wasn't what she'd bargained for when I asked her to marry me.

It took me a little more than a year and a half to finish college. Then I spent three years in seminary across the street, where I experienced the wonderful privilege of having my own father as my professor of preaching.

During my time of training, Angela also came to the point of surrendering her will and her life to Christ. She hurried home all excited from church one Sunday night to tell me what had happened. As we rejoiced together, she suddenly stopped and asked me, "This doesn't mean we're going to be missionaries, does it?"

I laughed and told her I didn't know.

As we neared the end of my last semester of seminary training, I firmly believed God had some sort of ministry in store for us. But I didn't have a clue what or where that might be. I shared my concern with a weekly prayer group of guys—asking them to pray with me that some door would soon open and the Lord would make his way obvious to me, and to Angela.

The very next day one of those men, my friend Joe, who'd been a college classmate my first time around, and was by this time a vice president of our alma mater, went to Indiana for a board meeting of a small but well-respected mission agency with fields of work around the world. One of the items on the board's agenda was a report on a new work that agency was just taking over from a sister organization in the West Indies.

My friend Joe perked up immediately when he heard that. He almost couldn't believe it when the speaker went on to say, "And the current ministry is centered in the U.S. Virgin Islands. But unfortunately, the couple serving there now will soon be returning to the States and will not be going back. At present, we don't know where we will find another couple with a heart for the people on the island of St. Croix."

Joe almost jumped out of his chair. But he managed to wait till the end of that session to approach the mission executive who'd made the report. The two of them called me that very night. And by the time we finished talking, I think we all felt the Lord was at work and had clearly opened a very exciting door.

So it was the next year, after further cross-cultural ministry training and more than a hundred meetings in churches and other Christian settings around the country, sharing our testimonies and our dreams for ministry in order to raise the funds needed to support our work, that Angela and I packed up our three daughters and our belongings to move overseas once again. This time our dreams and our motivations were very different from our first move to St. Croix, yet it seemed no less an adventure.

We couldn't have been any more excited than we now were to realize how God had been working in our lives to bring us to this place again at this time. How many first-time missionaries going overseas already feel as if they are finally going home? How many missionaries are going home? Literally, to move back into their own house?

The first time we'd moved to the islands, we'd been focused on our own dreams—seeking personal adventure and excitement. We'd been searching for more in life. And we'd found it.

But what made this second move to St. Croix even more exciting was our whole new perspective, which allowed us to see the bigger picture. We now realized that God, in his providence, in his prevenient grace, had been preparing us for this very ministry even before we had committed our lives to him. I was reminded of that Old Testament passage in Joel, a promise from God that my dad liked to paraphrase: "But I will restore unto you the years that the locusts have eaten." And so it was that God was restoring the years, using those decades that we were trying to run from him, to prepare us for a ministry many years down the road.

We could hardly wait to get started.

POSTSCRIPT

For the next eight years, my son Mark led a church-planting ministry in St. Croix — working mostly with native West Indians and recent immigrants from other Caribbean islands. Currently he works with indigenous Christian ministries around the world, offering short-term biblical, vocational, and leadership training for pastors and lay Christians. As he has shared his personal prodigal testimony in a variety of settings over the years, he has found that his story has opened new doors of ministry for him to "provide reassurance and hope for waiting parents (or grandparents) of prodigals."

What Mark's journey has taught me is that even if you feel you have reached the end of your rope of hope, there is still more rope. Even at our point of deepest despair, the Lord always has more options than we can ever see or imagine.

Most Christians, and all hurting parents, sometimes need to cling to that promise in Romans 8:28 where Paul assures believers not only that all things are possible with God, but that God can use all things — all unhappy circumstances, all great disappointments, all foolish or rebellious decisions, all discouraging situations, all painful hurts — so that they actually work for the good of those who love him. That is not to say he always delivers the happy endings we may wish and pray for.

But because our Lord, who is the same yesterday, today, and forever, isn't bound as we are by time and space, his all-things-work-together-for-good guarantee gives us great reason for hope. For that promise doesn't just apply to this day's overwhelming circumstances. God is not only with us in our current troubles. He is simultaneously at work — in our yesterdays (redeeming past mistakes, soothing old wounds, even healing painful memories and restoring those years the locusts have eaten), and in our tomorrows (planning and preparing a way for us to experience his goodness, grace, and purpose in a future we can neither imagine nor achieve on our own).

That is reason—for prodigals and their parents—to hope. That will be a future worth waiting for. And that will be my prayer, and my family's prayer, for you.

—Margie M. Lewis
Summer 2009

APPENDIX

Open my eyes to see wonderful things in your Word.
I am but a pilgrim here on earth: how I need a map—
and your commands are my chart and guide.
I long for your instructions more than I can tell.
—Psalm 119:18–20 TLB

Time after time as I have talked with parents, they have emphasized the role Scripture has played in guiding and encouraging them through their hurts. Many references have already been incorporated into this book. But this is an additional appendix of passages that have proved especially meaningful to the people who have contributed in the preceding pages.

"As for me and my household, we will serve the LORD" (Josh. 24:15).

"The LORD is close to the brokenhearted and saves those who are crushed in spirit" (Ps. 34:18).

"Trust in the LORD and do good; dwell in the land and enjoy safe pasture. Delight yourself in the LORD and he will give you the desires of your heart" (Ps. 37:3–4).

"Commit your way to the LORD; trust in him and he will do this: He will make your righteousness shine like the dawn, the justice of your cause like the noonday sun" (Ps. 37:5–6).

"Be still before the LORD and wait patiently for him; do not fret when men succeed in their ways, when they carry out their wicked schemes. Refrain from anger and turn from wrath; do not fret—it leads only to evil" (Ps. 37:7–8).

"Don't be impatient for the Lord to act! Keep traveling steadily along his pathway and in due season he will honor you with every blessing" (Ps. 37:34 TLB).

"For the LORD God is a sun and shield; the LORD bestows favor and honor: no good thing does he withhold from those whose walk is blameless" (Ps. 84:11).

"For the Lord is always good. He is always loving and kind, and his faithfulness goes on and on to each succeeding generation" (Ps. 100:5 TLB).

"But the lovingkindness of the Lord is from everlasting to everlasting, to those who reverence him; his salvation is to children's children of those who are faithful to his covenant and remember to obey him!" (Ps. 103:17 TLB).

"Those who sow in tears will reap with songs of joy. He who goes out weeping, carrying seed to sow, will return with songs of joy, carrying sheaves with him" (Ps. 126:5–6).

"Jehovah is kind and merciful, slow to get angry, full of love. He is good to everyone, and his compassion is intertwined with everything he does" (Ps. 145:8–9 TLB).

"Trust in the LORD with all thine heart; and lean not unto thine own understanding. In all thy ways acknowledge him, and he shall direct thy paths" (Prov. 3:5–6 KJV).

"You can be very sure that the evil man will not go unpunished forever. And you can be very sure that God will rescue the children of the godly" (Prov. 11:21 TLB).

"Reverence for God gives a man deep strength; his children have a place of refuge and security" (Prov. 14:26 TLB).

"Since the Lord is directing our steps, why try to understand everything that happens along the way?" (Prov. 20:24 TLB).

"Teach a child to choose the right path, and when he is older he will remain upon it" (Prov. 22:6 TLB).

"He will keep in perfect peace all those who trust in him, whose thoughts turn often to the Lord! Trust in the Lord God always, for in the Lord Jehovah is your everlasting strength" (Isa. 26:3–4 TLB).

"'As for me, this is my promise to them,' says the Lord: 'My Holy Spirit shall not leave them, and they shall want the good and hate the wrong—they and their children's children forever'" (Isa. 59:21 TLB).

"Thus saith the LORD; Refrain thy voice from weeping, and thine eyes from tears: for thy work shall be rewarded, saith the LORD; and they shall come again from the land of the enemy" (Jer. 31:16 KJV).

"Call unto me, and I will answer thee, and shew thee great and mighty things, which thou knowest not" (Jer. 33:3 KJV).

"Therefore I will look unto the LORD; I will wait for the God of my salvation: my God will hear me" (Mic. 7:7 KJV).

"For Christ promised [the Holy Spirit] to each one of you who has been called by the Lord our God, and to your children and even to those in distant lands" (Acts 2:39 TLB).

"They replied, 'Believe in the Lord Jesus, and you will be saved—you and your household'" (Acts 16:31).

"And we know that God causes all things to work together for good to those who love God, to those who are called according to His purpose" (Rom. 8:28 NASB).

"Do not be anxious about anything, but in everything, by prayer and petition, with thanksgiving, present your requests to God. And the peace of God, which transcends all understanding, will guard your hearts and your minds in Christ Jesus. Finally, brothers, whatever is true, whatever is noble, whatever is right, whatever is pure, whatever is lovely, whatever is admirable—if anything is excellent or praiseworthy—think about such things. Whatever you have learned or received or heard from me, or seen in me—put it into practice. And the God of peace will be with you" (Phil. 4:6–9).

CHECK OUT
THEHURTINGPARENT.COM

In addition to mission work equipping indigenous leaders of the church and coordinating construction for short-term mission trips around the world, I am also developing a broader ministry of reconciliation and healing for hurting families. Recently I have acquired rights to the web address TheHurtingParent.com to establish a resource to individuals, families, and churches. I'm convinced many congregations need to work harder and do better at being supportive communities, rather than condemning communities. I want to challenge and enable local churches and their members to move beyond judgment to extend grace to both prodigals and their parents.

A good starting point would be to carefully consider the most common possible reactions that my mother used as the chapter divisions of this book, first identifying and avoiding the most common negative responses — isolation, rejection, anger, guilt, and despair — and then working to foster those opposite, redemptive positive principles — fellowship, acceptance, unconditional love, forgiveness, and hope. Congregations and church leaders not only need to espouse and help parents apply these biblical principles; they need to be asking what parts of their existing local church program (e.g., prayer groups, Bible studies, Sunday school classes) might best minister to the hurting families in our midst.

So if you would like further information on this ministry, are interested in planning a Hurting Parent Seminar at your church, or want to contact us for any other reason, go to TheHurtingParent.com today.

— Mark Lewis

BIBLE VERSIONS

Scripture quotations marked KJV are taken from the King James Version of the Bible.

Scripture quotations marked NASB are taken from the *New American Standard Bible*, © Copyright 1960, 1962, 1963, 1968, 1971, 1972, 1973, 1975, 1977, 1995 by The Lockman Foundation. Used by permission.

Scripture quotations marked RSV are taken from the *Revised Standard Version of the Bible*, copyright 1946, 1952, 1971 by the Division of Christian Education of the National Council of Churches of Christ in the USA. Used by permission.

Scripture quotations marked TEV are from *Today's English Version—Second Edition*, copyright © 1992 by American Bible Society. Used by permission.

Scripture quotations marked TLB are taken from *The Living Bible*, copyright © 1971. Used by permission of Tyndale House Publishers, Inc., Wheaton, Illinois 60189. All rights reserved.

ABOUT THE AUTHORS

Margie M. Lewis was a pastor – seminary professor's wife for more than fifty years prior to her husband's death in 1996. She is a graduate of Asbury College and Asbury Theological Seminary and served for several years as executive secretary of the Asbury Theological Seminary Alumni Association. Her responsibilities in church and academic communities have given her numerous opportunities to minister to hurting Christian parents. She lives in Central Kentucky and has three sons, two daughters-in-law, and ten grandchildren.

Gregg A. Lewis is a son of Margie M. Lewis and the award-winning author/coauthor of more than fifty books — including such other Zondervan titles as *Take the Risk* with Ben Carson, *Forgiving the Dead Man Walking* with Debbie Morris, and the *New York Times* bestseller *Tom Landry: An Autobiography with Tom Landry*. Most recently, he and his wife, Deborah, coauthored the children's book *Gifted Hands: The Ben Carson Story* for Zonderkidz. Gregg and Deborah are parents of five adult children and live in Rome, Georgia.

Printed in the USA
CPSIA information can be obtained
at www.ICGtesting.com
JSHW030749230624
65200JS00005B/12